Michael's book made the process of applying for jobs sooooo much easier. **The way he broke down each part of both the cover letter and the résumé was sooo very helpful** and taught me so much that I never knew and definitely wouldn't have thought of. If you're not getting callbacks, confused, or simply want to improve your application presence, I definitely suggest getting this book to help with just that.

–Renee Reborn Browne, 5-Star Amazon Review

Job seekers can regularly refer to this handbook to gain useful tips that will lead them every step of the way through the maze of an employment search. This book is **concise, easy-to-read, and provides numerous examples** to support each recommendation. Highly recommend this book for all who are seeking to land their dream job!

–D. J. Sebastian, 5-Star Amazon Review

This was perfect. Short. To the point. Relevant and helpful. **I recommend.**

–T. A., 5-Star Amazon Review

Something they *don't* teach you in college is **how to ace an interview!** (At least, they didn't teach that to my son!) So I bought a copy for him . . . aaaand, I'll be using this for my daughter in high school and another son who is following an alternative-to-college path. I really love his attitude about seeking to serve when you're looking for a job that

alone **will make any applicant stand out.** And take note of his dad's "Philosophy of the Seven Ps"—it's priceless! A terrific addition to a homeschool mom's "guidance counselor toolbox"!

I believe this book can be for everyone, regardless if you are just starting out, fresh out of university, or have been laid off of work at the age of 55 and suddenly find yourself searching for a job. Without knowing how to **navigate through the current "job postings" and outmaneuvering the competition,** you'll find yourself at the back of the line.

This book is outstanding! **I highly recommend it to any young person in the job market.** I am going to make everyone I know who is in the job market aware of this must-have book. The author shows his own qualifications, then, in plain language, gives valuable systematic information on how to land that job! **Five stars are not enough.**

The author does an excellent job outlining **clear actionable steps for writing a résumé, forming a cover letter, interviewing, and more.** The author not only explains best practices but also gives great rationale for all that he presents, as well as includes some of his own story, **making for a fun read.** This book is a great tool for any job seeker!

–Michael Diettrich, 5-Star Amazon Review

If you are looking for a job or wanting to change jobs, you need this book! Michael Lachance gives "tried and true" strategies for taking any job seeker "from rejected to hired." He explains how to write a concise Cover Letter that is unique to each job application, write a Résumé that reflects the value you bring to a company, and specific tips on preparing for your job Interview. This book gives **step-by-step guidance** for writing each document and then gives a great example of each. **I feel this book is an essential, thorough, and proactive resource for any job applicant.**

–Celeste Allen, 5-Star Amazon Review

This book is an **easy read, well written, and gives clear direction** on the proper approach to writing a résumé and following up. Just seems so clear. **Should be a mandatory book for new grads.**

–Edyta L., 5-Star Amazon Review

This book changed my opinions and thoughts about how to market yourself for your dream job. It's a must read for every job seeker. I have discovered **so many unimaginable strategies** that can set you apart. You must market yourself very well and surpass the hiring manager's expectations.

Understanding the company's needs is the most important part of a successful job search. This wonderful book will give you all these solutions. I recommend it to everyone who wants to be successful in the actual job market.

–Amazon Customer, 5-Star Amazon Review

This book is an **easy, but informative read for both adults and students.** Michael conveys the most important aspects of the Job Hunt, Cover Letter/Résumé, & Interview process— **a great resource for students and high school Careers classes!** I highly recommend adding this to your collection!

–Steven and Kelli Koski, 5-Star Amazon Review

Land Your Dream Job

Join the 2% Who Make It Past Résumé Screening

Second Edition

MICHAEL LACHANCE

facebook.com/LandYourDreamJob

Paperback ISBN: 978-1-9990589-1-3

Get Your FREE Gift!

My mission is to empower you with total control over your employment destiny.

To get the best experience with this book, I've found that readers who download and use the

1-Hour Job Application Challenge

are able to implement faster and take the next steps needed to land your dream job.

Download the Challenge today by visiting:

bit.ly/lydjresources

Ps. Send this link to a friend who's looking to land their dream job. They'll thank you later ;)

Contents

Stay Connected With Michael:

On Facebook: **facebook.com/LandYourDreamJob**

On Instagram: **instagram.com/michance.11**

To get free Dream Job resources: **bit.ly/lydjresources**

To leave a review of this book on Amazon: **bit.ly/lydjreview**

INTRODUCTION

Now Is the Time to Land Your Dream Job

You're using the wrong strategy to land your dream job.

Even worse, you likely realized you used the wrong strategy after it was too late. You've already been rejected from the hiring process. And *now* you're asking for help to *get hired.*

Your parents, teachers, career counselors, and even some employment centers have *tried* to teach you how to apply for a job the *right* way. They know best, right?

They've told you the very first step to landing your dream job is to create a cover letter and résumé that describe you, your qualifications, and your skills. Include every last bit of experience—every qualification, every volunteer hour, every award you've ever received, just to make sure whoever reads your application *knows how qualified you are!*

Next, they told you to submit your application to every available job opening in town. In fact, they advised, send your application to any openings in the big city, too, because it's only an hour away, and there's *so much* potential there.

Then, they promised you that *someone* would get back to you and invite you for an interview. You went to school for all these years to be qualified for this position. You've performed so many duties that you're capable of doing pretty much anything. You're a "team player."

Why wouldn't you be the best candidate for the job?

And finally, after you were invited to the interview, you went in with more questions than answers, wishing you knew someone that just *knew what the heck actually happened once you got there.* Because every person who gave you job-search advice hasn't been in an interview themselves for years.

The strategy you've been taught is *wrong.* Unfortunately, you've learned rejection-worthy job-search strategies. In summary, the traditional job-search strategy plays out like this:

1. Create a cover letter and résumé (your application) that describe you and your skills.
2. Send your application to every available job opening in your city (and maybe another city, too).

3. Patiently wait to be invited to an interview (any day now, right?).

4. Go to the interview blind, with little preparation (what's it going to be like, anyway?).

You will not get hired using this strategy because, as the saying goes, you've put the cart before the horse. You've created your application before identifying the criteria the hiring manager will use to make a hiring decision. Criteria that will allow your application to stand out from the sea of other applications, criteria that will allow you to communicate your value in a way the hiring manager *understands.*

From Rejected to Hired

But now, there is an easy-to-read book with tried-and-true strategies that will lead you from rejected to hired. This book is for *you*, who is tired of waiting to get hired and who wants to be proactive and take control of your next job search.

Land Your Dream Job has been designed to walk you through every step of the job-search process, from reading and understanding the job description, to creating an effective application, to properly preparing for your interview.

This book is designed to provide both context and strategies so you know *why* you're implementing the suggestions I teach you.

Before you create an application for your dream job, you need to understand what the employer is truly looking for in an ideal candidate. Once you know the highest leverage experiences or skills the employer needs to see in your application, you can begin to create a targeted, results-oriented application.

The Winning Application Process

My dream job-worthy job-search process works like this:

1. Read and understand the job description or job scorecard to learn what's most important to the employer (Chapters 1–3).

2. Create an engaging cover letter, highlighting three to five specific skills from the job description or job scorecard (Chapters 4–8).

3. Create a professional résumé that focuses on results, using Achievement Statements (Chapters 9–13).

4. Properly prepare for your interview with practice questions and response techniques (Chapters 14–20).

Using this system, you'll create a strategic plan to apply for your dream job. You'll have clear objectives to work toward, and your entire application will be aligned to the employer's needs.

Proven Expertise

But who am I to teach you how to take control of your employment destiny?

I began helping job seekers land their dream job as a career assistant in 2009 at Brock University. In that role, I assisted students, alumni, and faculty to write cover letters and résumés for the jobs they were applying for. Each candidate's application was unique and required care to ensure the application matched the employer's requirements.

In that position alone, I reviewed and improved hundreds upon hundreds of résumés and cover letters in industries ranging from healthcare to education, from the applied sciences to law, from short-order cooks to bartenders and servers.

I helped them align their skills, experience, and degree with the job description to communicate the most critical information employers need to make a hiring decision.

At Brock, I was also professionally trained in interview strategies. I was taught how to prepare for an interview, how to respond to difficult questions, how to anticipate what questions would be asked, and what the interviewer *really* wanted to hear in my response.

I then used what I'd learned to interview job candidates who would take over my role as career assistant after I graduated. I've since used these skills interviewing job candidates in two other vastly different industries.

Waterville TG, Inc. is an automotive manufacturing company that specializes in weather stripping, or, to the average Joe, producing the plastic that goes around your windows and doors to keep water and wind noise outside of your car. I started at the company as a manual laborer and, in two years, I was promoted three times (I'll teach you the strategy I used to gain these promotions later in the book). I ended my tenure there two years ago as the Quality Control Lab Supervisor.

As the Lab Supervisor, I managed two lab technicians on day, afternoon, and night shifts. Our purpose was to perform tests like compression load deflection and coating thickness checks to ensure we met our customers' strict quality requirements and to reject product that didn't meet standards.

To ensure customer quality standards were maintained, I interviewed dozens of candidates who sought to work in the lab. Using the job description and understanding the purpose of the technician's role allowed me to interview and recruit (with the help of the HR department) the best-fit candidates for the position.

In my role as Student Success Representative at Self-Publishing School, I screened more than 550 job applications for a student success coach position. I then performed 30 screening interviews (high-level interviews to determine whether candidates are a possible fit for the role). By the time I finished, I provided a list of 10 A-level candidates to my manager. The leadership team hired two of the candidates from the list of 10 I provided my manager. The hiring campaign was a success.

This is all to say that not only have I been trained in industry-leading job-search techniques, but I've also used these techniques on both sides of the hiring table throughout my career. My experience extends beyond the scope of the "top-down" view of a hiring manager; it's also from the bottom up, meaning I've seen the hiring process through the eyes of both the hiring manager and through yours, the job candidate.

I promise you this: After being involved at this many interview tables, **I know what will help you land your dream job** (*and why you're getting rejected*).

If you're struggling to land a job, if you're aimlessly creating job applications that are not getting you invitations to interview, if you're transferring jobs within your company but have no idea where to start with your application, or even if you're exploring your employment options, you need to read this book!

It's time to stop cherry-picking advice from the Internet, from friends and family, and start creating a coordinated job application that will get you results.

Strategies and Tools

In this book, I give you a step-by-step walk-through of the entire application process, start to finish:

- Exactly what you need to get hired in the exact sequence you need to apply it
- Visual aids to help you create your application as you read this book
- The Achievement Statement formula to create impactful sentences for your résumé
- The Seven Ps philosophy to help you prepare for your interview
- A real sample of my own cover letter and résumé to prove this strategy really works
- Links to free resources including the 1-Hour Job Application Challenge and the real-life samples used in this book

Every one of the strategies presented will help you communicate your value as a candidate in a way the employer will understand. After using these strategies in her application, my cousin was invited to an interview in less than 24 hours. My sister has used these strategies to help land a job as a teacher, applying for and getting an interview in less than a week. Coworkers, ex-coworkers, LinkedIn˚ contacts, friends, friends *of* friends, classmates from university, random acquaintances, and community members—you name it—these strategies have helped people land jobs.

Whether you're wondering how to structure or what to include in your cover letter, or how to write effective sentences in your résumé, how to make your résumé professional, or what to include or not to include, this book is for you. In this book, you'll get answers to questions you don't even know you have yet.

"Moving up the corporate ladder" starts with getting your foot on that first rung at your new job—and I've helped countless job seekers achieve just that. I've supported everyone from candidates applying to their first part-time job, to students transitioning from university to full-time career, to seasoned employees making major career transitions. One thing is for sure: an effective application is the starting point to moving up the ladder.

After supporting so many job seekers over the past ten years, I decided to look into some job-search statistics and came across this quote from Robert Meier, President of Job Market Experts:

> *"**98% of job seekers are eliminated** at the initial résumé screening and only **the top 2% of candidates make it to the interview.**"*

In other words, you have a 98% chance of getting *rejected* in the hiring process. Only 2% make it past résumé screening. That's an alarming number of rejected applications!

So, what are the 2% of job candidates doing right?

To put it simply, they're giving employers what they need to make a hiring decision. They're positioning their cover letter and résumé to hit the bull's-eye of the employer's needs. They're communicating results, data, facts, and achievements throughout their application.

The thing is, I don't blame you for not knowing how to put together a rock-solid job application.

You haven't been taught how to use results and achievements to support your application. The people teaching you job-search strategies haven't applied for a job in years. They're providing outdated information that won't get you hired.

Whatever the problem is, no job means no paycheck, no career development, and no financial freedom.

I've seen the best of the best and the worst of the worst of applications. In this book, I'll guide you past the mistakes most candidates make in the job-search process and directly toward strategies that will get you hired.

You'll gain confidence with your application knowing you are providing employers what they need to hire you, not just a list of things you've done in the past (this is a *hugely* important strategy).

Everything you need to create a dream job-worthy application *today* is covered in this book. Plus, you'll have the chance to be a hero for someone in your life by passing on the free resources I'm about to share with you. (Who doesn't like to help the people they know?)

Open Doors of Opportunity

This book is a key that will open many doors of opportunity. You'll be empowered with the skills and ability to build a strategic application like never before. But doors of employment continually close, and employers want to fill job openings as quickly as possible.

Every day you wait to use this key is a day of opportunity you've given to another candidate—another candidate who is applying for your dream job *today*.

Don't lose out on another job opportunity due to inaction.

It's time for you to land your dream job and join the 2% who make it past résumé screening.

PS. Download the 1-Hour Job Application Challenge by going to **bit.ly/lydjresources**. There are *so many* golden nuggets in the book and I encourage you to read until the end, but if you're in a hurry, download the 1-Hour Job Application Challenge.

PPS. Share this book with a friend or family member. From my experience, job candidates don't ask for help when it comes to creating a job application. Creating a winning application is one of those things where everyone thinks they know how to do it, but no one really *knows*. They wait until it's too late, until after they've been rejected.

I know it, you know it, everyone knows it—*they need help.*

Send them to **bit.ly/lydjresources** to download free Land Your Dream Job content, including the 1-Hour Job Application Challenge.

PART I

JOB DESCRIPTION AND JOB SCORECARD

CHAPTER 1

Reading and Understanding the Job Description

When companies need to hire an employee, they create a job description for the position.

The job description (as the name implies) describes the general tasks or duties you may perform while on the job. It lists relevant information and requirements for the position, like years of experience, specific skills, and other qualifications. It may also include information such as the hours of work, job location, and salary range.

All the information you need to apply for the position is in the job description, including to whom to direct your application. Understanding the job description allows you to focus your cover letter on the skills, experience, and results that matter most to the company.

Following is a sample job description. Notice its four sections: the job description overview, duties, requirements, and how to apply.

Job Description: General overview of the position

Our client is currently looking for an experienced, accomplished, self-motivated Electrical Controls Engineer to lead in developing our products and systems. The Electrical Controls Engineer will work with a variety of functional groups that are directly involved in engineering, product development, implementation, and manufacturing partners.

Duties: Duties you can expect to perform in the position

- Evaluates electrical systems, products, components, and applications by designing and conducting research programs; applying knowledge of electronics, circuit design and software control.
- Confirms system's and components' capabilities by designing testing methods; testing properties.
- Perform detailed calculations to establish standards and specifications.
- Use computer-assisted engineering software (AutoCAD) to perform engineering tasks.
- Support Business Development with product development and testing.
- Develops electrical products by studying customer requirements; researching and testing materials, assemblies and systems.
- Performs system design, programming, simulation and testing using various software and protocols.
- Designs, modifies, develops, writes and implements software programming applications for embedded systems.
- Responsible for programming motion controls systems and the associated interfacing.
- Responsible for motor sizing, torque/speed calculations, and motion mechanism types.
- Assures product quality by designing electrical testing methods; testing finished products and system capabilities.
- Maintains professional and technical knowledge by attending educational workshops; reviewing professional publications; establishing personal networks; participating in professional societies.
- Contributes to team effort by accomplishing related results as needed.

Requirements

- Bachelor's Degree in Electrical Engineering Must-haves for the job
- 10+ years' electrical engineering experience
- Competent in the use of electrical engineering and control software (Labview, CAN, etc)
- Strong understanding of electrical manufacturing processes
- Able to problem solve and troubleshoot as the need arises

Application instructions, including Job ID

How to Apply

Interested applicants should submit their cover letter and resume outlining their qualifications to Brian at brian@hiring.com. Include Job ID 29471 in the subject line.

Use Targeted Keywords

A job description is like a grocery list of items that an employer is looking for in potential candidates. The more items on the grocery list the company can find in a candidate, the better. It is your job to show the employer you have most (not necessarily all!) of the items the company is looking for.

If you don't review the job description, you will not know how to focus your one-page cover letter. You could list every skill you possess, but unless you target specific keywords from the job description, you will not look like a good match for the employer.

The skills and keywords you use to focus your application will vary based on your experience, training opportunities, time in the workforce, and more. In Chapter 3, I'll explain how to effectively pull keywords from the job description, but for now, see the sample job description that follows.

If I had AutoCAD experience, created electrical software, designed electrical testing methods, and attended educational workshops, I'd focus on those specific keywords in my application.

Job Description:

Our client is currently looking for an experienced, accomplished, self-motivated Electrical Controls Engineer to lead in developing our products and systems. The Electrical Controls Engineer will work with a variety of functional groups that are directly involved in engineering, product development, implementation, and manufacturing partners.

Duties:

- Evaluates electrical systems, products, components, and applications by designing and conducting research programs; applying knowledge of electronics, circuit design and software control.
- Confirms system's and components' capabilities by designing testing methods; testing properties.
- Perform detailed calculations to establish standards and specifications.
- Use computer-assisted engineering software (AutoCAD) to perform engineering tasks.
- Support Business Development with product development and testing.
- Develops electrical products by studying customer requirements; researching and testing materials, assemblies and systems.
- Performs system design, programming, simulation and testing using various software and protocols.
- Designs, modifies, develops, writes and implements software programming applications for embedded systems.
- Responsible for programming motion controls systems and the associated interfacing.
- Responsible for motor sizing, torque/speed calculations, and motion mechanism types.
- Assures product quality by designing electrical testing methods; testing finished products and system capabilities.
- Maintains professional and technical knowledge by attending educational workshops; reviewing professional publications; establishing personal networks; participating in professional societies.
- Contributes to team effort by accomplishing related results as needed.

Requirements

- Bachelor's Degree in Electrical Engineering
- 10+ years' electrical engineering experience
- Competent in the use of electrical engineering and control software (Labview, CAN, etc)
- Strong understanding of electrical manufacturing processes
- Able to problem solve and troubleshoot as the need arises

How to Apply

Interested applicants should submit their cover letter and resume outlining their qualifications to Brian at brian@hiring.com. Include Job ID 29471 in the subject line.

Job descriptions have been around for years and have done a great job explaining the duties of a job. But, as Bob Dylan would say, "The Times They Are A-Changin'."

Job scorecards are becoming more and more common. In the next chapter, I'll explain what a job scorecard is and how you can use it to land your dream job.

CHAPTER 2

Reading and Understanding the Job Scorecard

When I worked at the Career Resource Centre at Brock University, it was common for employers to create a job description for an open position they were ready to fill. But these days, many companies are finding A-level talent by using job scorecards rather than job descriptions.

While a job description focuses on duties to be performed, a job scorecard focuses on the expected results or outcomes once in the role. A job scorecard outlines key performance indicators, or KPIs, and other required competencies needed to excel in the position.

KPI expectations are made clear early in the hiring process and are used to score or grade potential candidates when making hiring decisions. The job scorecard gives both the employer and employee an objective way to measure the success (or failure) of a new hire.

Another shift from the job description to the job scorecard is a new focus on culture. Companies of all sizes recognize that employees are happier and more loyal to the company's mission when there is a positive company culture. Therefore, fitting in with the culture is an increasingly common value indicator in the hiring process.

I cannot talk about job scorecards without giving the leadership team at Self-Publishing School (SPS) a huge shout-out for their work creating amazing job scorecards. Chandler Bolt, Founder and CEO of SPS, has a YouTube channel where you can find a video called "How to Create Job Scorecards for Your Employees." This video provides an amazing breakdown of the benefits of a job scorecard! I've also included a sample job scorecard for a marketing director position at Self-Publishing School at the end of this chapter.

Fitting the Company Culture

Maybe you've heard about the thought-provoking (and outlandish) questions Google asks job candidates to ensure a good culture match. If you haven't, you should Google, "interview questions at Google." The questions will blow your mind.

An interviewee might be asked, "If you could be remembered for one sentence, what would it be?" Or this one: "How many haircuts do you think happen in America every year?"

The purpose of asking questions like this (in my humble opinion, anyway) is to determine whether you fit the company culture. When faced with a difficult or odd question, do you give up easily? Or do you accept the question and do whatever it takes to succeed in giving a reasonable response?

Job scorecards include culture info because it's just *so* important to the success of the company.

Core Values

Before I was hired, two things about Self-Publishing School's hiring process stuck out and made me *really* want to work for this company (never mind the fact that I could finally come out of the closet as a full-on book nerd): An amazing company culture with a clear focus on *results*.

Self-Publishing School culture is defined by five Core Values:

1. Honesty and integrity always win.
2. Fail fast, fail forward, fail often.
3. Hard work and continuous self-improvement.
4. Everyone is responsible for facilitating change.
5. Best is the standard.

After viewing the company's core values, I thought to myself, "This is a company I *need* to work for."

Applicants who don't fit the culture need not apply. SPS doesn't waste time on the "wrong" applicants and instead focuses solely on attracting and hiring A-level talented people who fit the company culture.

Focus on Results

The second thing that stuck out was the clear focus on results. Because I understood the results that would be expected of me, I was able to decide whether I had the skills and experience needed to excel in the position. I could reflect on the results I achieved in the past to determine whether I had what it takes to be successful in this position. I was equipped with everything I needed to make a results-oriented application geared to what mattered most to the company.

In the next few pages, review Self-Publishing School's marketing director job scorecard. You'll notice it's very thorough, providing tons of behind-the-scenes information about the position, the company, and the culture. It even includes links to external resources applicants can use to research the company and improve their application.

With this information at your disposal, you can easily create a targeted job application using specific keywords (and results) the employer is looking for.

POSITION SUMMARY *Summary of the position*

This position is responsible for driving the economic engine at Self-Publishing School. Simply put, the purpose of this position is to reduce CTAC (cost to acquire customer) while also growing Self Publishing School's revenue as fast as possible.

This is done by managing the growth channels at SPS (see chapters 10 & 11 in Extreme Revenue Growth) and the leaders of those channels. There are 2 main ways to drive revenue:

1. Filling up the sales team's calendars with qualified appointments
2. Generating "non rep revenue" via marketing funnels

Research opportunity

When the job is done correctly, our most profitable marketing channels at SPS are growing quickly...with a high focus on doing more of what's working...thus reducing CTAC and growing revenue.

It's the role of the Marketing Director to focus the team on growing the channels that are working, prune the channels / campaigns that aren't working, and breed a culture of testing/innovation to sprout new marketing campaigns and channels.

All of these decisions are made by data and rigorous testing...NOT... "gut feel". Trusting your gut (informed by conversations with customers) is great when coming up with new tests to run...not when making big decisions on how to allocate marketing budget. 😊

You MUST be:

It's clear the company is looking for data-driven candidates. Application must be data-driven

- A great leader ready to lead a team
- Ready to learn, be challenged, and grow a ton
- Scrappy, and eager to get your hands dirty...working in the trenches with your team
- A systems thinker and numbers based decision maker
- An execution-oriented, results-based operator

Defining the "right" candidate

NOTE: This position full-time and virtual. Meaning you can work from anywhere. The team here at SPS is located around the world, with the majority of us in North America. Preference for this position is someone working in the US or Canada.

Defining the "wrong" candidate

DISQUALIFIERS: Please DO NOT apply to this position if you:

- Have no interest in books (and using books to change people's lives)
- Aren't willing to get your hands dirty / get in the weeds with marketing campaigns, implementation, etc
- Have zero experience leading a team

If none of these things can be said of you, then please continue reading...

Requirements

At Self Publishing School, we value work ethic, coachability, and past results you've delivered significantly more than your degree (or lack thereof), GPA, etc.

Have you delivered results in a similar role in the past? If so, that's what we're looking for.

That being said, feel free to apply even if you don't "tick the boxes" below. Just be sure to mention that in your application + why we should consider you.

Required:  Summary of minimum requirements

- You've run the marketing team for a company doing at least $3M/year (or were the right hand person)
- More than 3 years of marketing experience
- Ability to create & grow multiple marketing channels (and manage the leaders of those channels) in a way that drives down CTAC while also growing revenue
- A visionary with a deep understanding of innovative online & offline marketing strategies and a proven track record of creating campaigns and initiatives that will drive down CTAC while increasing revenue.
- A strong leader / executive who can lead a team
- Thorough hands-on-keys experience building, implementing, and maintaining marketing campaigns and automated systems.

Preferred: Ideal level of experience

- Experience running marketing for a company doing at least $20M+ in annual revenue (or the right hand for that person)
- More than 6 years of marketing experience

Benefits

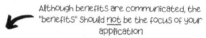 Although benefits are communicated, the "benefits" should _not_ be the focus of your application

Yearly salary of $70,000 – $140,000; depending on qualification and experience.

Also includes the following benefits:

- **Top tier healthcare:** your choice of high quality healthcare (for US-based full-time employees)
- **Bi-weekly house cleaning:** get your house cleaned every two weeks, on the company! :)
- **Work remotely:** save $5k/year in commuting costs and 100+ hrs each year (aka. 2 ½ extra weeks of "time off")
- **Participation in the company profit share**

About the culture:  Self-Publishing School Culture

Here are the company core values. We call it "The SPS Way":

1. Honesty & Integrity Always Win
2. Fail Fast, Fail Forward, Fail Often
3. Hard Work & Continuous Improvement
4. Everyone is Responsible for Facilitating Change
5. Best Is The Standard

Click here to watch a video from our founder Chandler Bolt explaining the company Core Values.

Although the team is virtual at SPS, the culture is alive and well...often referenced as one of employee's favorite parts about working here.

2-3 times a year the team meets in a unique city in the US (sometimes internationally) for a 3-5 day company retreat...planning the next quarter, connecting in person, having fun, and celebrating wins.

The environment is very fast paced, and high growth. The company is growing fast, meaning a high level of accountability, responsibility and autonomy for everyone on the team.

We're constantly investing in the training & growth of our team members through book clubs, courses, trainings, and live seminars. All employees are given $15,000+ worth of training and continued education upon being hired with the company. ← Major focus on training

Since you're working remotely, you can say goodbye to the dreaded commute (meaning more time for family & fun). This isn't your average 9-5. Hours are somewhat flexible as long as you get your work done. That being said, due to the growth & pace of the company, it's not uncommon to work 40-50+ hour weeks.

Because of the company's growth & hiring needs, there's a huge opportunity for advancement and promotion if you're a fast learner.

Overall, the culture of the company is high growth, fun, empowering, and motivating, with support from a world-class team of people who love what they do.

In 2019, Self Publishing School was certified as a "Great Place To Work" by GreatPlaceToWork.com. ← Research opportunity

Click here to watch a video from our CEO (Chandler Bolt) on how we build GREAT culture on our virtual team at SPS. ← Research opportunity

Now that you know the difference between a job description and a job scorecard, I have a task for you to help you focus your application on what matters most to the company you're applying to.

CHAPTER 3

Job Description / Job Scorecard Action Plan

Take a few minutes to complete this action plan. These steps are critical if you're to create an effective, targeted job application. Plus, you'll need the items you create now to complete the job application you'll be building throughout this book.

1. Print the job description or job scorecard for the job you are applying for.

   o   Yes, actually print it.

2. Underline any "required" certifications or experience.

   o   These are must-haves for the employer and need to be referenced in your cover letter and résumé.

3. Out of the remaining "preferred" skills and experience listed, ask yourself:

   o   What items provide the most value to the employer?

- o What items have the most impact toward the success of the role?
- o What items do I have the most experience doing?

Underline three to five items.

- o These are the certifications, skills, and experience you will target in your cover letter and résumé.
- o Skills beyond your top five do not deserve to take up room in your cover letter.

4. Take note of any special instructions like application deadline, who to direct your application to, job ID, and any other requested information to include in your application.

- o You will need this information later.

Not aligning your job application to the skills requested in the job description or job scorecard is why most candidates don't make it past résumé screening. So, keep the job description or job scorecard and your notes handy as you move to the next chapter to begin writing your cover letter.

PART II

COVER LETTER

CHAPTER 4

What Is a Cover Letter?

Landing your dream job starts with building a strong cover letter. In this chapter, I'll explain what a cover letter is so that you understand why you're creating one in the first place.

A cover letter is a one-page document used to entice an employer to hire you. It's the first document a hiring manager will look at, along with your résumé, as part of your job application. It consists of four main sections. Its purpose is to illuminate your passion and desire for the position while highlighting your most relevant qualifications for the job.

Make Every Sentence Count

Before I walk you through what needs to go in each paragraph of your cover letter, I'd like to share a few important points with you.

Your cover letter may be the only thing a hiring manager will *ever* read about you. It's critical to make every sentence in your cover letter count toward marketing yourself and your skills. Hook your future boss's attention by showing how your experience will bring value to the company.

Align Your Skills

One of the most common mistakes I see when reviewing cover letters is that candidates do not match their work experience with the required skills of the job. You need to be sure that you align the skills or experience the company needs with your own related skills and experience in your cover letter.

For example, a company may seek strong accounting skills, but the candidate focuses his cover letter on serving as captain of his school's varsity sports team. That's great experience but doesn't show how the candidate can fill the company's specific need.

In this case, the hiring manager needs accounting skills. So, the candidate's job is to articulate why and how his accounting skills are exactly what the company needs.

Failing to communicate accounting experience will get that application tossed in the reject pile!

Focus on the Company's Needs

Explain what you can do for the employer, not what the employer can do for you.

The company is the Alpha in the hiring process—they dictate terms, and your job is to give the company what it asks for. The job search process is all about give, give, give. As soon as you mention what *you'll receive* in this job (like saying you'll receive biweekly house cleaning, or you'll no longer have to commute to an office), your chances of getting the job are drastically reduced.

Include Keywords

Companies want to hire as quickly and efficiently as possible. But, finding and recruiting new employees is an exhausting and time-consuming process.

In fact, many companies use software to scan through job applications to search for specific keywords. This step makes the process of finding candidates with the required skills even faster because applications that don't fit the company's criteria are excluded from review.

The problem is, many candidates don't include skill keywords in their cover letter and résumé. From the software's perspective, these candidates do not have the skills or experience the company needs.

Follow Instructions

This software can scan for other items, too. Most job descriptions include a job number. If the job number isn't in your cover letter, you won't get hired because the software doesn't know what job you're applying for.

One job scorecard I've seen asked candidates to include a weird phrase in the cover letter. The company would filter the applications using the phrase and would quickly know which candidates were capable of following instructions.

But have no fear! You won't make any of these costly mistakes.

Now that you know what a cover letter is and how hiring managers will use it, we can move on to why it's so important for you to have a cover letter no matter what job you are applying for.

Chapter 5

Why You Need a Cover Letter

If you apply for a job without a cover letter (even when it's not requested), you're significantly decreasing your chances of landing the job.

I can promise you that someone else in the applicant pool will submit a cover letter with their application. That candidate's cover letter will put their work experience into context in ways that your stand-alone résumé never will. In truth, you're making it easier for the next candidate to get this job.

Customize Your Cover Letters

I'm grateful for the varied employment experiences I've had over the years. But one thing was always certain: I had to create a brand new cover letter for every job I applied for. If I used the same cover letter with every job application, I would not have been maximizing my potential in explaining why I would be a good fit for each role. Some of those positions required different skills or certifications that the others didn't.

If I wanted to get hired, I knew that I had to create a new cover letter for each position.

Put Your Skills Into Context

Yes, you need to write a new cover letter for every job you apply for.

It doesn't matter if you're applying for a new job, for a promotion, or even to work for an old boss—the rule is the same. You need a customized cover letter that focuses your application on the required skills for the position. If a company is looking for skills X, Y, and Z, a strong cover letter will explain the results you've achieved using skills X, Y, and Z.

No Exceptions

When I worked at Brock University, I applied for a supervisor position (a promotion) in the Career Resource Centre. In the new position, I would work for the same boss, sit in the same seat, but would be in a leadership role. Nothing in my work environment would change. Even so, I wanted to prove to my manager I had the skills and experience it would take to be a leader in this new position. I did that in my cover letter.

I created a new cover letter when I applied for a promotion at Waterville TG Inc., too. I would work for the same boss.

Yet, I wrote a new cover letter to demonstrate that I had the skills and work ethic to deserve the promotion. I didn't want anyone else to get that job because I didn't put my skills into context. I had to prove I had the skills my manager needed in this new role.

Creating a new cover letter for every job I applied to—even when applying to the same company—allowed me to put my value into context.

I received a promotion in both cases.

Now that you understand why it's so important to create a new cover letter for every job you apply for, it's time for you to learn the foundations of a cover letter.

CHAPTER 6

The Structure of a Cover Letter

A well-structured cover letter will give your future employer a great first impression of your organizational skills. A badly structured cover letter will leave whoever reads it either underwhelmed or indifferent. It's as simple as that.

To land your dream job, you need to put forth the effort to make your letter perfect. Ignoring the tips I'm about to share may result in the hiring manager throwing out your application simply because you lack the organizational ability to communicate your skills. First impressions last, and you want to make sure you knock this first impression out of the park.

A quote from one of my favorite TV shows, *Suits*, reiterates my point. The ultra-savvy, world-class lawyer Harvey Specter tells his then-naive associate, Mike Ross, "If you start behind the eight-ball, you'll never get in front." To stay in front of the eight ball—and in front of all other candidates—you need a kick-ass cover letter. So, let's get started.

Just One Page

A cover letter is a one-page document. No more, no less. Use the letter as an opportunity to put your work experience into context for your future employer. Because it's written in paragraph form and directed to the hiring manager, a cover letter is more personal than a résumé.

I'll discuss what goes into each section of your cover letter in the next chapter. But know that your cover letter will have four sections:

1. The company's contact information
2. The introductory paragraph
3. The main body where you'll communicate your skills
4. The closing paragraph

Nothing More

Because the purpose of a cover letter is simple—getting an interview—do not make your cover letter more confusing than it needs to be by adding extra paragraphs or including information that does not belong.

One page. That's it. No extra bells and whistles, no spinning rims, and no Gucci Gang.

Let's quickly consider the following scenario. Say a hiring manager is comparing your cover letter to another candidate's. Your information is well-structured, easy-to-read, and organized into three paragraphs on a single page. Meanwhile, the other candidate's cover letter uses a variety of fonts, includes jumbled information, and is three pages long.

I promise you this: Employers want candidates who efficiently communicate their value. The one page, concise, and effective cover letter will win over the disjointed, three-page document every time.

Great things come in small packages. Quality over quantity. Less is more.

These are philosophies used by uber-successful companies. Take the hint and use these strategies in your application.

What Not to Include

Now that you understand the basic structure of a cover letter, let's discuss a few things you should *not* include in your cover letter (or résumé).

Do not include pictures in your cover letter or résumé. Do not include information regarding marital status, sexual preference, religious affiliations, or political leanings. Unless necessary for the position you're applying for, these topics do not speak to employment skills or experience.

If you're honest about creating a targeted, effective cover letter for the job you're applying for, you need to focus on what will get you the job.

***

International candidates applying for work in North America, take note: While other cultures may encourage including profile pictures and age when applying, this is not a requirement in the North American job market and may, in fact, play into the hiring manager's biases.

***

Now you know the importance of a great first impression, the structure of a cover letter, and what not to include in your cover letter. In the next chapter, you're going to start writing your cover letter.

CHAPTER 7

How to Write Your Job-Worthy Cover Letter

It's time to create a cover letter for your dream job!

To recap, a cover letter has four main sections:

1. The company's contact information
2. The introductory paragraph
3. The main body where you'll communicate your skills
4. The closing paragraph

The Company's Contact Information

Let's get started on section one of your cover letter.

At the top of a new Microsoft® Word doc or other word processor (personally, I use Google Docs™), type today's date. Under the date, leave a line space, and then type the contact information of the company (found on the job description or job scorecard):

Use this for reference:

Today's date

Company's name
Company's street address
City, State/Province, ZIP/Country code

Leave two lines blank below the company's contact info. Direct your cover letter to the hiring manager you've researched or found on the job description or job scorecard.

For example, "Attn: Michael Lachance."

If you don't know the hiring manager's name, pick up the phone and call the company to find out. The little things, like using the hiring manager's real name, matter. From a hiring perspective, it shows you've done your research and that you're proactive. You're clearly taking this job search seriously. You've shown initiative.

Many candidates do not do their research and will simply write, "To Whom It May Concern." Doing so tells me you don't have the initiative to pick up the phone, call, and ask for the hiring manager's name. This is uncharacteristic of a hard-working employee. I find it hard to believe you'll contribute results to the company if you can't pick up the phone.

And remember, some companies use programs to filter through the applications they receive. If you don't include the manager's name, he or she may never know your application even exists.

The Introductory Paragraph

Section two of your cover letter is your introductory paragraph. It should be three sentences long. Leave a blank line and get started.

In the first sentence, tell the employer what job you are applying for. If there is a job number on the job description or job scorecard, include it here.

In the second sentence, include one or two skills, certifications, or educational experiences you have that will stand out to the employer. Capture the employer's attention and give the company a reason to continue learning more about you.

In the third sentence, state that you have the experience and skills needed to excel in this position. Make it obvious. Explain how you will benefit the company and bring value to its team.

***

If you were referred to this position by someone who already works for the company, include his or her name in the introduction section of your cover letter. Referrals go a long way when it comes to getting hired.

***

The Main Body

Section three of your cover letter is where you target the skills from the job description or job scorecard and further explain how your experience addresses those needs.

Refer to the three to five skills or experiences you identified in Chapter 3 and appreciate how important it is to target these specific skills.

Imagine you are a baseball player at home plate, ready to take a swing at a pitch. In this analogy, the pitch is the job skill, and you want to connect the pitch with your personal experience and value to hit a home run. The only way for you to get a home run is to show the employer how you will apply your experience toward the skills the company needs.

Whenever possible, use quantitative measurements to best express your value.

If you've improved a Net Promoter Score* via customer service improvements, use the NPS score increase to provide a quantitative measurement of success.

If customers filled out feedback surveys, use numerical feedback to show you've improved the customer service experience.

Numbers are objective, measurable, and the best weapon you have when creating an effective job application.

In the same way, continue to address the rest of your three to five skills or experiences in this paragraph. The entire paragraph needs to focus on the employer's specific needs.

To provide you an example for this section of the letter, I'd like to share a cover letter I used in my application to the Ontario Provincial Police (OPP). (You can find the complete letter in Chapter 8.) Some candidates waited months for an interview with the OPP, but I was invited for an interview in only a few weeks.

Although I got an interview for the constable position, I didn't get hired as a police officer. I did end up taking a role that I'm much better suited for, that I love, and fulfils me. Either way, I like to believe my strong cover letter was among the reasons I secured an interview so soon.

My sister and I grew up around police officers. We saw firsthand how the police work with the public in all kinds of ways. While officers find most interactions with the public rewarding, some experiences can be difficult and demanding. To be ready for the unexpected, police officers must have strong communication skills.

But rather than simply saying "I have communication skills" in my cover letter, I spoke about how I used those skills to provide value to my employer at that time. I wrote:

> Five years ago, I began employment with Waterville TG as a laborer. Within a short time, I was promoted to Quality Control Specialist, where I represented Waterville across North America. In that position, I minimized quality issues by actively listening to customers, identifying their needs, and implementing countermeasures. My communication skills allowed me to work fluidly with many departments and levels of management.

In only a few sentences, I highlighted my personal and professional development resulting from my communication skills.

Aside from what I found in the job description, I did a lot of research to learn more about the OPP. I wanted to know— inside and out—its mission, core values, struggles, and successes policing communities in Ontario. I learned that the OPP values engaged members of the community, continuous self-improvement, and continued education.

I came out strong in my cover letter by stating that within a few years, I went from a manual laborer (entry-level position) to Quality Control Specialist (management role)— a perfect example of personal and professional growth.

The OPP places a lot of value on professionalism, too. The promotions I received (and subsequent supervisory experience) spoke to the value I place on setting a professional example for my colleagues. To demonstrate how I value professionalism, I continued:

> Two years ago, I was promoted to Quality Control Laboratory Supervisor. This position was a big challenge because the lab had not been managed before. Yet, I used this opportunity to demonstrate my leadership abilities along with my desire to take on a challenge. I now supervise more than nine lab technicians and have overseen multiple audits with zero nonconformances.

Here I'm showing that I had a major challenge in front of me: taking over an unmanaged lab. But within a short time, I supervised more than nine lab techs while upholding quality control standards, resulting in zero nonconformances.

There is a theme of continuous improvement—one of the OPP's core values—in my cover letter. Police officers continually participate in training activities throughout their careers. In my cover letter, I demonstrated how I continuously push myself toward a bigger challenge and more responsibility. I used every sentence as an opportunity to prove that I have the character and experience the OPP finds valuable.

The Closing Paragraph

Section four of your cover letter is your closing paragraph. It should be three sentences long.

First, thank the employer for considering your application. Second, encourage the employer to contact you via the best phone number and email address to reach you. Third, invite the employer to learn more about you by reading your résumé.

Lastly, leave a single blank link space and on the next line type, "Sincerely," followed by your signature and then your typed name.

I also suggest typing "Enclosed: Résumé (2)" at the very bottom of the page (if you have room). This tells the employer you have two (2) résumé pages that go with your cover letter.

Completely necessary? Maybe not. But it subtly shows your professionalism and organizational skills. And what employer doesn't value these skills? They all do!

Proofread!

It's time for the least enjoyable, but arguably one of the most critical parts of the application process: Proofreading!

Read your cover letter aloud—not just in your head. When you read it in your head, your brain automatically corrects errors and makes sentences flow better than they really do. If your letter sounds bad when your future employer reads it, you will not be moving forward in the hiring process.

After you read it aloud and make any needed adjustments, look carefully for any typos, spelling errors, or grammar mistakes. Because it can be difficult to identify mistakes in your own writing, this might be a good time to ask someone with good language skills to check your letter for errors. Again, you will be passed over for the job for these simple mistakes.

In Chapter 8, you can see the complete sample cover letter I wrote. You can also download a copy of my cover letter at **bit.ly/lydjresources**. Use my cover letter as a reference while creating your own. Observe the format and spacing between the different sections of the sample letter.

After you've reviewed the sample letter in Chapter 8 and have completed your own cover letter, you can set it aside for now. In the next several chapters, we're going to shift gears and focus exclusively on résumés. You'll learn how to create an achievement-focused résumé that will communicate tangible value to your future employer.

CHAPTER 8

Sample Cover Letter

[Today's Date]

Police Academy
123 Police Avenue
City, State/Province

Attn: Officer Carl, Uniform Recruitment,

It is with confidence and pleasure that I apply for a constable position with the Ontario Provincial Police. I have demonstrated many of the OPP's core values in my tenure at Waterville TG and in my role as Quality Control Laboratory Supervisor. I firmly believe that my ethical character, employment experience, and life experience make me a strong candidate for this position.

Five years ago, I began employment with Waterville TG as a laborer. Within a short time, I was promoted to Quality Control Specialist, where I represented Waterville across North America. In that position, I minimized quality issues by actively listening to customers, identifying their needs, and implementing countermeasures. My communication skills allowed me to work fluidly with many departments and levels of management. Two years ago, I was promoted to Quality Control Laboratory Supervisor. This position was a big challenge because the lab had not been managed before. Yet, I used this opportunity to demonstrate my leadership abilities along with my desire to assume a challenge. I now supervise more than nine lab technicians and have overseen multiple audits with zero nonconformances. My current role also includes supervising document control as well as ensuring that proper testing methods and failed test procedures are followed. My ability to succeed is in part due to my experience as an Aboriginal Career Assistant at Brock University. My Métis origin allowed me to work with Brock's Aboriginal population in career development and to provide culturally specific programs. Outside of work, I have an active social life, play sports in the community, and have served as a volunteer with the Red Cross and Sarnia-Lambton Rebound. All these experiences have inspired me to make a real and positive impact on my community.

I invite you to view the rest of my résumé, which provides more information with regard to my employment and volunteer history. I can be contacted to schedule an interview via email at michancebooks@gmail.com or by cell phone at (123)456-7890. Thank you for your time and consideration.

Sincerely,

Michael Lachance
Enclosed: Resume (2)

PART III

RESUME

CHAPTER 9

What Is a Résumé?

A résumé is a professional document used to showcase your employability when applying for a job. It includes your education, employment, and volunteer achievements. To help further describe who you are as a professional candidate, it also can include awards and certifications you've received.

An achievement-focused résumé matches your unique experience and skills to the company's needs from the job description or job scorecard. Achievements or results can be any quantitative impact you've made to a company's bottom line. Providing achievements and results in your résumé shows your ability to accomplish tasks and contribute to the company's success.

List of Duties—NOT

You will *not* land your dream job listing duties on your résumé.

A common mistake that job candidates make is listing only the duties or tasks performed at a job. Listing a duty such as "tracked inventory" or "fulfilled customer orders" does not paint a picture of how you brought value, results, or achievements to the company. The hiring manager will not see any value in you as a candidate, and you will not be hired.

You are a great time manager. So what? What did you achieve by being a great time manager? Did you set a record for speed of service times? Did you save the company money by reducing production time? Did you beat a deadline that allowed you to start another project a month ahead of schedule?

The most important thing to communicate is the *result* of your actions.

Two Types of Résumés

There are two common types of résumés: Chronological and Functional.

Each type has its own strengths and weaknesses. I don't want to spend a lot of time diving deep into each one, but knowing a little about each may help you determine the best way to show your experience.

A Chronological résumé lists employment history in reverse chronological order so your most recent work experience is listed first and your earliest experience last. Every employment position on your résumé is an opportunity to highlight specific skills and keywords from the job description or job scorecard. Every work and volunteer experience, award, and certification is listed in chronological order on my résumé.

A Functional résumé is a little less common. It lists skill sets in functional categories such as marketing or project management to create industry-specific themes. This type is most beneficial when you have a lot of experience in one industry, and the company is looking for a candidate with a lot of experience in that one thing.

Regardless of the type of résumé being used, when the hiring manager picks up yours, that person needs to be immediately attracted to what you offer. Otherwise, the hiring manager will throw your résumé to the side and never look at it again.

About Promotions

Job candidates want to get hired faster. The thing is, there *is* a way to get hired faster.

The more promotions you receive, the easier it is to get more promotions down the road—and get hired faster.

Companies do not promote employees with a lousy work ethic. They *will* promote employees who show up and work hard every single day, who make smart decisions, who are great team players, and who encourage those around them.

No matter where you work now—whether it's at a local coffee shop or at a major bank—set your sights on a promotion. Getting a promotion now makes it easier for a company to hire you in the future.

The hiring manager will see promotions in your application and will understand the commitment and loyalty you had to your previous employers. The companies trusted your judgment and gave you increasing amounts of responsibility.

Every time you get a promotion, you take on a bigger leadership role, learn the managerial systems that come with it, learn to communicate better, and learn to supervise others—among many other leadership, managerial, and transferable skills.

Improving these skills makes you a stronger candidate. It sets you apart from the people who have been working for the same length of time but have not received a promotion.

From a hiring perspective, career advancement tells the hiring manager that you have a proven history of doing what it takes to succeed.

Be Ready

One way to ensure the hiring manager *does* read your application as soon as possible is to keep your work experience on your résumé up-to-date.

Today's economy, including the jobs created by it, is in a major transition. For many candidates, experience from 10 or 15 years ago may no longer be relevant. Therefore, try to keep the experience listed on your résumé within the last 5-10 years and relevant to the position you're applying for.

You now understand the DNA of a résumé and have learned the secret to promotion success. Next, it's time to briefly talk about why you need a résumé to land your dream job.

Chapter 10

Why You Need a Résumé

In the preceding chapter, we explored what a résumé is, how to use it effectively, and how receiving a promotion can help you get hired faster. Now it's time to discuss why you need a résumé and how you can use it for maximum effectiveness.

Every single job seeker on planet Earth needs a résumé. Companies and recruiters need your résumé to make a hiring decision because it represents you and the value you'll contribute to their company. They cannot make a hiring decision without understanding who you are as a professional candidate.

Your résumé is the single most effective tool in the hiring process for helping you land a job.

Once your résumé is brought to life, you can repurpose it to expand your presence into online job-search communities. The achievements, results, and value you've contributed in the past will be twice as effective by proactively communicating your skills on LinkedIn.

You owe it to your future employer—and yourself—to make getting hired as easy as it can be for all parties involved. And it starts with your résumé.

Customize It

Like your cover letter, your résumé needs to be customized for every position you apply for. Tailor each résumé to highlight the skills needed for each job.

Can creating customized résumés be time-consuming? Sure, it can!

But do you know what's even *more* time-consuming? Being unemployed! Or being stuck in a position you don't love. Or being surrounded by negativity in a toxic work environment.

Every application sent that is *not* customized is another day lost from building a credible employment history. In the end, you lose time, money, and the happiness you deserve.

Ain't nobody got time for that!

Résumés and LinkedIn

Before moving on, let's be honest with ourselves: How long will résumés even last? And what other resources are out there to help with your job search?

Résumés will be around for a long time—whether they are printed on a few pieces of paper or in a file on your computer ready to be sent at a moment's notice. And now, LinkedIn has cemented itself as the next big advancement in the job search marketplace.

When you're done reading this book, you'll have all the content you need to create a professional presence online. If you don't have a LinkedIn profile yet, I highly encourage you to create one.

On LinkedIn, employers will be able to learn more about you amongst the sea of applicants, and headhunters will find you based on your experience, employment history, achievements, and endorsements from coworkers.

You'll also find many job opportunities. Not only will you be offered recommendations for jobs that relate to your education and skills, but you'll also be able to follow companies you'd like to work for and hear about opportunities as soon as they become available.

Applying Online

I mentioned this earlier but it bears repeating: hiring a candidate is time-consuming.

Reviewing a candidate's application is tedious, especially when there are multiple documents that need to be reviewed. This means that companies will use every opportunity to cut costs and increase efficiency to avoid sucking manpower into the hiring process.

In fact, many organizations now *only* accept digital applications, including police services like the Ontario Provincial Police.

Rather than collecting paper copies of cover letters and résumés, school transcripts, reference letters, awards, certificates, driver's licenses, and birth certificates, the OPP requests these documents to be submitted electronically as a PDF.

The idea that you *need* to submit your cover letter and résumé in person, on paper, is no longer true.

In the next chapter, I'll teach you how to structure your résumé, step by step. Let's get started.

CHAPTER 11

The Structure of a Résumé

The professional structure of your résumé will give your future employer a great first impression of your organizational skills. On the other hand, a disorganized and badly formatted résumé may, fairly or unfairly, lead a hiring manager to believe your work ethic is disorganized, too. This is a big reason why 98% of people don't make it past résumé screening. Fair or unfair, first impressions last.

When structured properly, your résumé will be easy to read and will allow the employer to determine whether you'd be a good fit for the company.

Be Consistent

Use consistent formatting in your résumé.

Consistency in every section of your résumé is so important. Consistency is organized, and organized is professional. This is the most overlooked, yet most impactful strategy you can apply to your résumé right now.

Consistent formatting means:

- Job and volunteer position titles are the same size and bolded.
- All indentations are in the same position throughout your résumé.
- Section headers are the same size, caps-locked, underlined, and boldfaced. Use no more than two font styles, and not any of the fancy ones.
- The spaces between section headers and position titles are the same.
- Every date on your résumé is aligned at the far-right side of the page.
- Every bullet point is the same format (use round black bullets).

These may seem like small details—but that's what makes them important. Your résumé is a professional document. But if it doesn't look professional, why should an employer consider hiring you?

Format your résumé correctly and set expectations that you intend to be organized and professional from the very beginning of the hiring process.

Include Section Headers

Following are the common section headers in a résumé. Note that Professional Development, Certifications, and

Awards sections are optional. Include them only if you have meaningful experience you want to communicate to the employer.

The section headers are usually displayed in this order:

- Contact Information
- Education
- Employment Experience
- Volunteer Experience
- Professional Development (optional)
- Certifications (optional)
- Awards (optional)

Although it would be nice to see your personality shine through your résumé by adding your picture or a few friendly emojis, do not include them. This is a professional document meant to entice a hiring manager to hire you. North American companies don't want or need your photograph unless specifically requested.

Align the Dates

I can't stress how important formatting is, so I'd like to focus on date alignment once more.

Align every date from your education, employment experience, volunteer experience, awards, and certifications at the far-right side of the page.

You may think it's silly and no one will notice if the date is not completely aligned at the far-right side of the page. They will notice. Don't be that sloppy person!

Pay Attention to the Details

Your résumé is like a painting, and each sentence is a single brushstroke. Pay attention to every detail and prove you'll bring this detail-oriented work ethic to the company.

Two Pages or Less

Keep your résumé to two pages or less. If your résumé is three pages long, skim through your experiences and find something to remove. Delete the least important details. If you need three pages to explain why you deserve this job, you're not focusing on what's most important to the employer.

Maybe you have sentences that don't speak to the most important skills you need. Perhaps you've included an employment experience that is not at all relevant to the position you are applying for. Employers don't have time to go through your application with a fine-toothed comb. Keep only what is most valuable to the employer.

Track Your Versions

Lastly, keep track of résumé updates by naming your résumé files like this:

Last name_First name_Resume_Dec_2019

The latest update was in December of 2019. The information in this résumé should reflect all education, work experiences, volunteering, awards, and certificates up to this date.

Few candidates think to create professional names for their résumé files. Most names are a random assortment of characters and don't clarify what the file contains. I don't know about you, but I don't open files if I don't know exactly what's inside.

Another way you can name your résumé file is by the job you are applying for. This makes it easy to know what industry-specific skills you are highlighting in your résumé.

Now you understand the blueprint of your résumé. It's time to start building it.

CHAPTER 12

How to Write Your Job-Worthy Résumé

In 2019, Self-Publishing School received more than 550 applications for a student success coach position. It was a huge number of applications—way more than we anticipated, and too many to review each one thoroughly. So, like many companies, we used a system to screen them.

The résumé screening process is like a chopping block for résumés.

The first thing we had to do was cut down the applicant pool to a manageable size. We needed a system to take the number of applications from more than 500 to say, 25. Using information from the position's job scorecard, we filtered the applications so we could focus on the most worthwhile (and results-oriented) candidates.

My goal now is to empower you with the tools that will help you get past résumé screening. Let's get started!

Contact Information

Everything the employer needs to contact you goes inside the Contact Information section. Use the Header section of a blank Google doc and center align the text.

1. On the first line, type your first and last name. Bold the text and increase the font size. Your name will be in the biggest text size on your résumé.
2. On the second line, type your street address, city, state or province, and ZIP or country code.
3. On the third line, type your phone number and email address.
4. On the fourth line, use the underscore key to create a horizontal line that will serve as a visual break between your Contact Information and your Education section.

Use the following image for reference, or go to **bit.ly/lydjresources** to download my most up-to-date résumé sample.

Michael Lachance
Address, City, Province/State, Postal/Zip Code
Cell: (123) 456-7890 Email: michancebooks@gmail.com

Remember, no hiring manager wants to take more than a few seconds to find your contact information. This format is clean, professional, and will help you land your dream job.

Education Section

Bold, underline, and caps lock the word **<u>EDUCATION</u>**. This is your Education section header.

Leave a single blank line underneath.

1. Next, type the most recent education degree you've received and bold the text.
2. On the same line, aligned at the far-right side of the page, type the date range of when you went to school for this degree.
3. On the next line, use the bulleted list format and type the name of the university, college, or high school you graduated from, including the city and state or province.
4. Repeat this process for all the degrees you intend to list on your résumé.

Some job candidates have asked me, *What should come first, the name of the degree or the name of the school?* In most cases, employers list a degree as a requirement for the position they're hiring for. They do not require the degree to come from a specific school. Therefore, list your degree first.

When you're done, your Education section should look like the following sample.

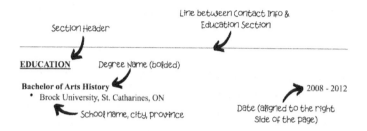

Control the Controllables

I need to make a quick (and massive!) shout-out to Chandler Bolt, CEO and Founder of Self-Publishing School. He has an amazing YouTube channel called "The 7-Figure Principles Show". One video in particular, "Control the Controllables," is a must-watch, especially when it comes to things like aligning dates at the right-hand side of the page.

Controlling the controllables is about recognizing what you *do* have control over (e.g., aligning dates at the right side of the page) and what you do not have control over (e.g., whether you will be invited for an interview).

You do not have control over whether you get hired, but you do have complete control over your application.

In nearly every résumé I've reviewed, date alignment is inconsistent or disorganized. For example, the date is next to the degree in the Education section but is in the middle of the page in the Employment Experience section.

Overall, inconsistent and disorganized date alignment can make an otherwise professional résumé look, well, ugly.

Control the controllables and align those dates at the right edge of the page!

Employment Experience

Bold, underline, and caps lock the words **<u>EMPLOYMENT EXPERIENCE</u>**. This is your Employment Experience section header.

Leave a single blank line underneath.

1. Next, type your most recent job title and bold it.
2. On the same line, aligned at the far-right side of the page, type the date range of when you began and ended employment for this job. If you are still working for this company, type "Present" instead of an end date.
3. Underneath your job title, in regular font, type the name of the company you work(ed) for, including the company's location (city and state or province).

This is what your Employment Experience section should look like so far.

Achievement Statements

Most candidates are rejected from the hiring process because they do not include achievements or results in their résumé. These candidates list the duties they performed but not the results their actions had on the company's bottom line.

When hiring a candidate, hiring managers make educated decisions based on factual information. Whenever possible, you need to provide them with quantitative results that prove you are a strong job candidate.

In your application, quantitative data can include conversion percentages, revenue increases, expense decreases, sales numbers, response times, grade levels, Net Promoter Scores, or any other numerical data that shows clear results.

To emphasize this point, check out Chandler's opinion on the need to include quantitative results:

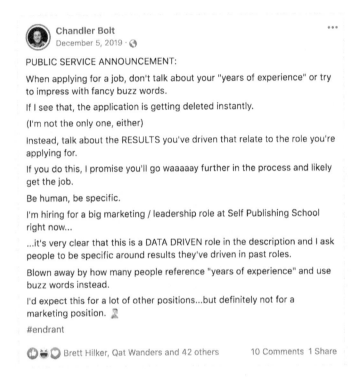

Chandler Bolt
December 5, 2019 ·

PUBLIC SERVICE ANNOUNCEMENT:

When applying for a job, don't talk about your "years of experience" or try to impress with fancy buzz words.

If I see that, the application is getting deleted instantly.

(I'm not the only one, either)

Instead, talk about the RESULTS you've driven that relate to the role you're applying for.

If you do this, I promise you'll go waaaaay further in the process and likely get the job.

Be human, be specific.

I'm hiring for a big marketing / leadership role at Self Publishing School right now...

...it's very clear that this is a DATA DRIVEN role in the description and I ask people to be specific around results they've driven in past roles.

Blown away by how many people reference "years of experience" and use buzz words instead.

I'd expect this for a lot of other positions...but definitely not for a marketing position.

#endrant

Brett Hilker, Qat Wanders and 42 others   10 Comments 1 Share

Provide the hiring manager with the most impactful data needed to hire you, in the form of Achievement Statements.

Achievement Statements allow you to communicate each achievement or result you've accomplished in a structured sentence. Each job you include on your résumé should have three to five Achievement Statements, and ideally, each statement will focus on a result listed in the job description or job scorecard.

Introducing the Achievement Statement formula:

Action word (past tense) + **context** (what you did / who you did it for) + **achievement** (results you achieved)

The Action word is a single word used to describe the core function of what you did. The Context explains what you did and who you did that action for (e.g., the company or the people you were serving). The Achievement is the objective or quantifiable results of your actions.

In my experience, most candidates write only the first and perhaps the second piece of this formula. They state their action, or what they did. Some candidates go as far as saying who they did it for. But there is no result or achievement, and no understanding of the impact they had on the company they worked for.

To help you communicate your achievements, ask yourself these questions:

- Do you work hard to save your customers, or the company you work for, time and money?
- Do you find ways to increase efficiency?
- What key product indicators (KPIs) are you responsible for? How have you improved them?

- What specific value do you provide, and to whom?
- How did you improve the customer's experience this year?
- How do your actions contribute to the company's growth?

Use the answers to these questions to create results-focused sentences that target what matters most to the employer.

Following are a few examples of Achievement Statements from my résumé to help you create yours.

EMPLOYMENT EXPERIENCE

Student Success Representative   March 2018 – Present
Self-Publishing School, San Francisco, California
- Created a Self-Publishing School Help Center that reduced the number of Support Tickets for the Student Success team by more than 90%
- Refined an Accounts Receivable campaign, resulting in $15,000 in past-due collections every month
- Systematized daily procedures and activities to increase efficiency, which merited the 2018 "Playbook Beast Q4" award in recognition of those efforts

As you can see, there are no vague, general statements like, "Helped Self-Publishing School customers." Instead, there is a clear result of each one of my actions, with context.

Let's break down the Achievement Statement formula using the examples I just provided:

- Created (**action word**) a Self-Publishing School Help Center (**context**) that reduced the number of Support Tickets for the Student Success team by more than 90% (**achievement**)

72

- Refined (**action word**) an Accounts Receivable campaign (**context**), resulting in $15,000 in past-due collections every month (**achievement**)
- Systematized (**action word**) daily procedures and activities to increase efficiency (**context**), which merited the 2018 "Playbook Beast Q4" award in recognition of those efforts (**achievement**).

Achievement Statements allow the hiring manager to use objective data to make an informed decision on whether you are a good fit for the position. Write Achievement Statements for every Employment Experience you intend to include on your résumé.

This strategy is *so* effective, yet so few job candidates even know about it.

Do you have a friend who's currently looking for a job?

Tell them to go to **bit.ly/lydjresources** to help them land their dream job by downloading free Achievement Statement resources. They'll thank you later!

Volunteer Experience

Bold, underline, and caps lock the words **<u>VOLUNTEER EXPERIENCE</u>**. This is your Volunteer Experience section header. Include this section if you have volunteer experience that would be valuable to the employer.

Leave a single blank line underneath.

1. Type your most recent volunteer position title and bold it.

2. On the same line, aligned at the far-right side of the page, type the date range of when you began and ended volunteering for this organization. If you are still volunteering, type "Present" instead of an end date.

3. Under your volunteer title, in regular font, type the name of the organization you volunteer(ed) for, including its location (city and state or province).

Each volunteer position you include on your résumé should have two or three Achievement Statements, and ideally, each sentence should focus on a result listed in the job description or job scorecard.

Once again, here is the Achievement Statement formula:

Action word (past tense) + **context** (what you did / who you did it for) + **achievement** (results you achieved)

The Action word is a single word used to describe the core function of what you did. The Context explains what you did and who you did that action for (e.g., the organization or the people you were serving). The Achievement is the objective or quantifiable results of your actions.

Following is the Volunteer Experience section of my résumé for your reference.

VOLUNTEER EXPERIENCE

Choices Program Volunteer   March 2018 – May 2018
Sarnia-Lambton Rebound, Sarnia, ON
- Dedicated 2 hours weekly to support Sarnia-Lambton Rebound and positively impact local community
- Engaged in positive discussions with youth, focusing on substance abuse, prevention, and intervention techniques to help them make more informed decisions

Let's break down the Achievement Statement formula using the examples I just provided:

- Dedicated (**action word**) 2 hours weekly to support Sarnia-Lambton Rebound (**context**) and positively impact local community (**achievement**)
- Engaged (**action word**) in positive discussions with youth (**context**), focusing on substance abuse, prevention, and intervention techniques to help them make more informed decisions (**achievement**)

Before moving on, write Achievement Statements for all the volunteer opportunities you intend to include on your résumé.

Professional Development

Before you continue reading, I'd like you to know that the sections you include in your résumé may vary from mine depending on your experience and the qualifications you'd like to include in your application. If you don't have any professional development to include in your résumé, you may want to choose workshops, awards, or certifications instead of professional development. You can even opt for a combination of titles like I've done in mine.

Bold, underline, and caps lock the words **<u>PROFESSIONAL DEVELOPMENT</u>**. This is your Professional Development section header. Include this section if you have completed training or have certifications that are required by or would be valuable to the employer. Professional certifications, aptitude tests, language tests, publications, job-related training, health and safety training, and advanced qualifications can all go here.

Leave a single blank line underneath.

1. Next, type the name of the most recent training you've received or have been certified in.
2. On the same line, aligned at the far-right side of the page, type the date of when you received the training or were certified. Include only the year unless the certification is time-bound to a month.
3. Repeat this process for any other professional development certifications you intend to include on your résumé.

Here is the Professional Development section of my résumé for your reference.

PROFESSIONAL DEVELOPMENT/WORKSHOPS

Michael Hyatt's "The Focused Leader" Training	2019
Copywriting Mastery - Digital Marketer HQ	2018
Student Success TedX Talk - Presentation Training	2018

Awards

Bold, underline, and caps lock the word **AWARDS.** This is your Awards section header. Include this section if you have room left on your résumé and have received an award that would be valuable to the employer or would speak to your character inside or outside of the workplace.

Leave a single blank line underneath.

1. Next, type the name of the award you've received most recently.
2. On the same line, aligned at the far-right side of the page, type the year you received the award.
3. Repeat this process for any other awards you intend to include on your résumé.

Here is the Awards section of my résumé for your reference.

AWARDS

Best is the Standard Award – Self-Publishing School Core Values Award	2019
Facilitating Change Award – Self-Publishing School Core Values Award	2018
Honesty & Integrity Award – Self-Publishing School Core Values Award	2018

References Available Upon Request

At the very bottom of the last page of your résumé, type "References Available Upon Request."

But before submitting your application, create a list of three references to use in the hiring process. Most companies like to speak to at least three references before making a hiring decision. They will likely request that you submit your list of references either before or during the job interview.

Be sure to ask each reference for permission to be included in your list of references and let them know that they may be called to provide details about your personal and professional history.

A **personal** or **character reference** is someone who can speak to the hiring manager about your character outside of the workplace. That person can vouch for the value you bring and can describe your personality and abilities.

A **professional reference** is someone you have worked with who can speak to your character in the workplace. This should be someone who understands your professional work ethic.

Avoid using your parents or good friends as a reference because there may be an obvious conflict of interest. If your parent is your boss or supervisor, find someone else within the organization to speak to your skills. And if you have no references at all, get out and volunteer!

The hiring manager will need to know how to contact your references. In a new Word or Google doc, type the word "References" and center it at the top of the page. Provide the following information for each reference:

- First and last name
- Relationship to you (personal or professional?)
- Position title and the company the person works for
- Email address
- Phone number

Bold each reference's name so it's easy to pick out. This will also establish a visual break between your list of references.

Here is an example of how your references should look.

References

Chandler Bolt
Professional Reference
CEO & Founder of Self-Publishing School
Author of *Published.: The Proven Path From Blank Page to Published Author*
emailaddress@gmail.com
(123)456-7890

Omer Redden
Professional Reference
Product Manager at Self-Publishing School
Author of *Life Doc: How to Succeed in Life Without Losing Your Faith, Family, and Friends*
emailaddress@gmail.com
(123)456-7890

There you have it!

You've now created a résumé worthy of landing your dream job.

I'm super-confident you'll be part of the 2% that makes it past résumé screening!

Exciting, isn't it?

In the next section, I'll show you how to prepare for your interview.

But first, check out my résumé sample on the next two pages. Use it as a reference to make sure your résumé is structured correctly.

Chapter 13

Sample Résumé

Michael Lachance

Address, City, State/Province, Postal/Zip Code
Cell: (123)456-7890 Email: michancebooks@gmail.com

EDUCATION

Bachelor of Arts History 2008 – 2012
- Brock University, St. Catharines, ON

EMPLOYMENT EXPERIENCE

Student Success Representative March 2018 – Present
Self-Publishing School, San Francisco, California
- Created a Self-Publishing School Help Center that reduced the number of Support Tickets for the Student Success team by more than 90%
- Refined an Accounts Receivable campaign, resulting in $15,000 in past-due collections every month
- Systematized daily procedures and activities to increase efficiency, which merited the 2018 "Playbook Beast Q4" award in recognition of those efforts

Quality Control Lab Supervisor January 2016 – March 2018
Waterville TG, Petrolia, ON
- Trained and supervised more than nine lab technicians on three separate shifts to ensure proper quality control measures are adhered to
- Audited the quality control lab on a regular basis to verify that lab jigs and other quality equipment matched control plans and customer specifications
- Developed operating and troubleshooting instructions for lab technicians to ensure technicians could problem solve on their own before escalating any concerns

Quality Control Specialist October 2013 – January 2016
Waterville TG Group, Petrolia, ON
- Provided support and training to production team members in the interpretation of product quality, fit, and functions
- Managed external customer complaints by investigating concerns, implementing countermeasures, and revising PFMEAs with quality engineers
- Maintained quality documentation, improved standard operating procedures for quality, and participated in daily meetings to ensure WTG met customer quality specifications
- Revised and updated control plans on a regular basis to ensure Ford, Honda, Toyota, and GM parts conformed to customer specifications and engineering standards

Michael Lachance

Address, City, State/Province, Postal/Zip Code
Cell: (123)456-7890 Email: michancebooks@gmail.com

Senior Career Assistant   May 2011 – April 2012

Career Services, Brock University, St. Catharines, ON

- Developed resources, including a Career Paths for Teachers binder that allows students to find career-related information specific to their program
- Worked collaboratively with the Resource Coordinator and Faculty Liaison to plan, coordinate, and deliver career-related projects and events for the academic year
- Facilitated weekly meetings and managed daily email and walk-in statistics to ensure that service goals were met on a weekly and monthly basis
- Presented workshops on a job-search database called GoinGlobal in front of large audiences, while also introducing students and alumni to job-related resources
- Interviewed students applying for Career Assistant positions and made recommendations for new hires, while also ensuring their continued success by mentoring new coworkers

VOLUNTEER EXPERIENCE

Choices Program Volunteer   March 2018 – May 2018

Sarnia-Lambton Rebound, Sarnia, ON

- Dedicated 2 hours weekly to support Sarnia-Lambton Rebound and positively impact local community
- Engaged in positive discussions with youth, focusing on substance abuse, prevention, and intervention techniques to help them make more informed decisions

PROFESSIONAL DEVELOPMENT/WORKSHOPS

Michael Hyatt's "The Focused Leader" Training	2019
Copywriting Mastery – Digital Marketer HQ	2018
Student Success TedX Talk – Presentation Training	2018

AWARDS

Best is the Standard Award – Self-Publishing School Core Values Award	2019
Facilitating Change Award – Self-Publishing School Core Values Award	2018
Honesty & Integrity Award – Self-Publishing School Core Values Award	2018

References Available Upon Request.

PART IV

JOB INTERVIEW

CHAPTER 14

How Proper Prior Planning Will Prevent a Piss Poor Interview Performance

You now have a cover letter and résumé that will get you past a company's screening process. It's time to prepare for your interview so you can land your dream job!

Let's start off with a philosophy my dad, Mitch, has pounded into my head over the years. It's super helpful as you prepare for your interview. This philosophy is called the Seven Ps; and while he used it a lot when coaching me in hockey, the philosophy of the Seven Ps can be used to win at life itself.

The Seven Ps are:

Proper **P**rior **P**lanning **P**revents **P**iss **P**oor **P**erformance.

Proper prior planning will prevent you from giving a piss poor performance. And because it's never too early to prepare for your interview, why not start right now?

It may seem like obvious advice but landing your dream job means not having a piss-poor interview. The problem is that most candidates do not prepare for their interview nearly as much as they should. When the day comes, Peter Procrastinator ends up feeling stressed and anxious because he has not properly prepared.

Follow the Seven Ps, and I guarantee you will stand out from the pack, even if your education and work experience doesn't.

Anticipate the Questions

How can you properly prepare to participate in this potentially positive meeting? It starts with anticipating the questions! Just like you anticipate problems in the workplace, you need to anticipate what interview questions will be asked so you can start preparing responses.

What are your strengths? What are your weaknesses? I have asked, and been asked, these two questions many times. You have not properly planned (and will have a piss-poor interview) if you're unable to answer these questions immediately.

Start brainstorming how you can answer these questions while focusing on the employer's needs. If the company is looking for a team player, speak to strengths you have working as part of a team. If the company is looking for someone who is organized, be ready to provide a few examples of your organizational skills.

Turn Your Weakness Into a Strength

Communicating your weaknesses can be a little trickier than talking about your strengths. You don't want to outright state you are terrible at a specific task or mention you have no experience using a skill the employer needs most.

Instead, state a weak skill you possess, but don't stop there. Go on and describe how you've taken action to improve that skill. If you prepare this answer properly, you'll be able to turn your weakness into a strength. Here's an example of how to communicate a weakness:

My organizational skills used to hold me back from getting promotions. Notably my ability to coordinate projects from start to end. So, I chose to work with my mentor to improve my project management skills. I've now led three major projects that were so well organized, they went off without a hitch and thoroughly impressed my manager. In fact, we've seen an increase in sales, and customers are more engaged than ever.

This response clearly identifies a weakness, acknowledges its negative impact, and communicates what steps have been taken to improve.

Prepare Some Responses

By now, you may be asking, *How the heck can I anticipate questions for a job I've never worked at?* It's a great question!

My answer: Google it!

Start by searching, "interview questions asked at [company name]." You're very likely to come up with some relevant questions to ask, and you can start practicing immediately.

Next, I suggest you review the three to five skills you pulled from the job description or job scoreboard. Because these skills appear in the job description or job scorecard, you can bet your bottom dollar you will be asked about them. So, use the job description or job scorecard to prepare to speak about these topics during the interview.

Questions for the Interviewer

At the end of your interview, you'll be asked whether you have any questions for the interviewers. This is an opportunity to learn more about the company, show your interest in the position, and stand out from other candidates.

I encourage you to prepare at least two meaningful questions to ask the employer. For example, ask what an average day looks like at the company or how the company culture is embraced every day. Inquire about the company's approach to solving a major problem, or how the company defines success.

Show your enthusiasm for the job by having these questions prepared ahead of time.

Be Genuine

Most interviewers will not waste time with trick questions or purposely try to stump you. So, try not to be nervous. Be yourself.

Answer the questions honestly. Admit when you don't meet the criteria for what the company is looking for. If you are a driven and competent individual, you may get away with not having a few qualifications if you fit the company culture.

Admit where you are weak, over-deliver where you are strong, and you will land your dream job.

By doing proper prior planning, you will certainly not have a piss-poor performance. Your purposeful preparation will make you a perfect applicant for this position. Let's pitter patter, pal!

CHAPTER 15

Practice Before Your Interview

Online tools and freelance services available on the Internet will help you prepare for your interview. These tools include programs like InterviewStream, InterviewFocus, freelance mock interview services on Fiverr, or by reaching out to me personally on the Land Your Dream Job Facebook page. Whatever tool you choose, I highly recommend that you participate in a mock interview.

The purpose of a mock interview is to give you an opportunity to practice your interview skills before your actual interview. Much like a real interview, you'll be asked a variety of questions specific to the job you're applying to.

Ideally, the mock interview is recorded. After you answer questions from the interviewer, you can go back and review your responses. From there, you can reflect on how to improve delivery of your responses as you prepare for the real thing.

You may feel silly, all alone, speaking to yourself on webcam. That's okay. I know how it feels because I have used InterviewStream (and participated in mock interviews) many times myself. But the sooner you embrace the self-analysis and self-criticism that you'll inevitably experience in the mock interview, the better.

Practice, Practice, Practice

Do not wait until your interview to test yourself under pressure. Search Google for one of the services I recommended here to get started. Or, ask a friend or colleague to help you perform a mock interview. In the next chapter, I provide a variety of questions you can use to start practicing with.

Having resources like InterviewStream—where you can do mock interviews in the comfort of your own home—is a gift for the modern job seeker. And the fact that you can do this in your bedroom while no one else is around is empowering.

At hockey practice, to build strong and natural habits, you put yourself into situations you will face during a real game. You learn how to respond to different situations and gain an awareness of how different scenarios can play out. Practicing gives you strength during games.

Lucky for you, most candidates don't practice. They think they already know the answers. They believe they can perform on the spot when the time comes. Or they simply don't take this process seriously. In the end, the person who goes in cold will lose to the candidate who is prepared and clearly articulates his or her experience and value.

Evaluate Yourself

After recording your mock interview, watch the video and evaluate yourself.

What are you communicating? Are you responding to questions using the skills listed in the job description or job scorecard? Are you speaking to the skills you highlighted in your cover letter and résumé?

If not, try practicing again. The company needs a candidate who has the specific skills listed in the job description or job scorecard. You need to speak to these skills during the interview. So, if you're not doing this on InterviewStream, try again.

As you continue to observe your responses, note the following:

- **Body language.** Your posture can say a lot about you. As much as possible, sit up straight. It shows confidence. An interview is no place for slouching.

- **"Um" or "uh."** Listen for how many times you say "um" or "uh." When you're asked a question, instead of saying "um" or "uh," pause for a few seconds or say, "That's a great question, let me think about that for a second" before responding. A 5-second break to collect your thoughts is a lot better than saying "um" throughout the entire interview.

- **Tone of voice.** Employers want to see confidence, character, and excitement from you. Why would they want to hire a monotone robot? Put some excitement in your voice while you practice! Show the company the excited tone you'll bring to the position after you're hired.

- **Breathing.** Be aware of your breathing habits. I've seen many candidates get anxious during an interview. Their breathing quickens, and soon they are out of breath as they try to answer the questions. Learning how to control your breathing will go miles in helping you rock this interview.

Now that you have a better understanding of how to prepare for an interview environment, let's discuss specific questions you can prepare for.

CHAPTER 16

Types of Interview Questions

Mock interviews will help improve your communication techniques and body language. Now you need some questions to prepare for. The more targeted your response to a question, the better your odds of landing your dream job.

This chapter covers some of the most common questions asked in an interview. If you can answer these questions effectively, you will be miles ahead of your competition. Trust me—few people can answer these questions as coherently as you might think. More times than I care to admit, I've asked a question that candidates were unprepared for. They stammered, incoherently, providing few relevant details about their employment experience.

I don't want you to make the same mistakes.

These candidates could have been incredible employees. But the fact that they couldn't answer a few simple questions took them out of the running. They didn't follow the Seven Ps and prepare for the interview seriously enough.

Market Yourself

So how can you prepare more effectively, knowing that every answer you give will be rated against the responses of the other candidates? You can start by repeatedly asking yourself:

- Why should this company hire me instead of another candidate?
- What do I have that provides the most value for the company's needs?
- Why do I want this position? What about this company makes me the most excited?

These questions can be tough because we typically don't enjoy marketing ourselves and our skills. The thing is— that's exactly what you need to do at your job interview.

Speak to experiences that relate to the job description, the job scorecard, or the company's mission, goals, and objectives.

There are two common types of interview questions. The key is to understand that different types of questions exist, and the approach to answering them is slightly different.

Behavior-Based Questions

The first kind is the **behavioral-based question.** Behavioral-based questions explore your behaviors when dealing with different situations from your past. In the hiring manager's mind, your past behaviors foreshadow future behavior. Understanding how you dealt with a past problem may suggest how you will respond to a similar situation in the future.

Following are 10 common behavioral-based interview questions. Even though you'll tell a story from your past, respond in a way that will provide value to the employer in the future.

1. Give an example of a time you faced conflict while working as part of a team.

2. What do you do if you disagree with someone at work?

3. Have you ever made a mistake at work? How did you handle it?

4. Give an example of a time you had to take on the role of a leader.

5. Tell me about a time you worked effectively under pressure.

6. Describe a time you didn't meet the expectations of your manager.

7. Have you experienced a stressful situation? How did you deal with it?

8. Share an example of how you were able to motivate employees or coworkers.

9. Have you ever gone beyond the call of duty? If so, how?

10. How do you handle a challenge? Give an example.

For each question, prepare stories about behaviors from your past. Even if you're not asked these specific questions, you'll have several stories to relate during the interview that illustrate your value.

Competency-Based Questions

The second type of interview question is the **competency-based interview question.** These questions determine whether you have the experience and skill for the job you're applying for.

For these questions, you'll need a solid understanding of the skills listed in the job description or job scorecard. Think of the different experiences, jobs, and environments in which you've used the skills the employer is looking for. Then prepare to speak directly to those skills while answering competency-based questions.

Following are 10 common competency-based interview questions:

1. Give an example of a time when you led a team. What did you accomplish?

2. Describe a time you've used effective time management to complete a project.
3. Tell me about a time you failed to complete a project on time.
4. Tell me about a time your communication skills helped improve a situation.
5. Tell me about a time you responded to negative customer feedback.
6. Describe a situation where you had to deal with an angry customer.
7. Describe a time you performed a task you'd never done before.
8. What is your biggest achievement?
9. Tell me about a time you failed to communicate properly. Looking back, what would you have done differently?
10. Give an example of a time you identified a new approach to a workplace problem.

If you can answer these questions effectively, you will be miles ahead of the competition.

Use the STAR Method

To maximize the value of your responses, use the STAR method. This method can be very effective in helping you structure your responses, and it breaks down as follows:

Star: Describe the Situation.

Task: Describe the Task required of you.

Action: Describe the Actions you took.

Result: Describe the Results of your actions.

First, you describe the problem or situation you were facing. Next, you explain the task, or what you had to do to correct the situation. You then explain the actions you took to make the change happen. Finally, you describe the results of your actions.

Notice how this process is similar to the way you built your Achievement Statements. This method communicates your experience in a way the employer will understand. It also keeps the results of your actions at the front of your mind for each question you answer.

Practice Some More

Practice answering these questions the same way as any other professional—through repetition.

Professional athletes, police officers, soldiers—you name it. They never stop training. If you genuinely want to land your dream job, practice, and then practice some more. Otherwise, you will lose out to the candidate who took the time to practice before the big game.

I have now equipped you with practice interview questions to help you prepare. You also have an effective, results-focused method for answering questions.

Next, I want to show you how you can prepare even further to truly live by the Seven Ps. Let's talk about what you should and shouldn't wear to your interview.

CHAPTER 17

Dress to Impress

This chapter is all about what you should (or should not!) wear to your interview. How you dress will lend insight into how well you've prepared, how seriously you're taking the job interview, and your level of professionalism.

Although most job interviews happen in person, telephone and video interviews (using software like Skype or Zoom) are becoming more common. Regardless of the type of interview you're participating in, I recommend using my Dress to Impress strategy—whether the interviewer will "see" what you're wearing or not. Dressing professionally, even for a phone interview, will provide you with confidence that is so important, especially when the interviewer isn't able to read your body language.

This is my Dress to Impress philosophy when it comes to what to wear to an interview:

Look good. Feel good. Play good.

This is a motto I have stood by for most of my life.

Look Good

Every time you get dressed up nice and fancy, you feel like a rock star, right? Like when you dress for a wedding. The gents spend extra time shaving until their faces are as smooth as a baby's bottom. Ladies spend most of the morning in the bathroom applying makeup, getting their hair done, and painting those nails.

Once we're prepared, we look good enough to strut down the red carpet. A bunch of badasses, right? We look good!

Feel Good

When we look good, we feel good.

Think back to the last time you were at a wedding. Everyone had an extra boost of confidence, right? Extra pep in their step, some extra swagger in their . . . strut? Everyone is surrounded by great-looking people with big smiles, and excitement is all around us.

We feel good!

Play Good

When we feel good, we play good.

We have more confidence in these moments not only because we are celebrating marriage, but because we have put ourselves in that positive mindset. When we look our best, we project happiness with our body language. Dressed for success, we are on our A-game.

We know we look our best, so when we see a cute gal or guy, we confidently swagger right up and ask for a dance. We dance like no one's watching, using moves we didn't even know we had.

This same attitude comes into play when you prepare for an interview. Build that confidence before you even walk into the interview. Look good. Feel good. Play good.

Dress for the Job You Want

The rule of thumb is to dress for the job you want. Every interaction with the employer is an opportunity to display your deep desire for this job. If you are applying for an entry-level position but you really want a supervisory job, dress as if you are applying to be a supervisor.

The minimum standard is business casual.

But what does business casual actually mean? Business casual does not mean dressing casually, as the name may imply. Business casual does not mean dressing up in a casual outfit (say, jeans and a collared short-sleeved shirt). What it means is dressing down a business outfit (suit pants, long-sleeved collar shirt, no tie).

Your clothes should be clean and wrinkle-free. The goal is to look professional, put together, and neat. And I promise you, when you look professional, put together, and neat, you'll truly be living by the philosophy of Look good, Feel good, Play good.

Put Some Effort Into It

Whatever you wear to your interview, you are foreshadowing the effort you'll bring to the company and customers. First impressions matter here, too.

Men should wear dress or khaki pants with a pair of black or brown loafers (these are good colors to have because they can match pretty much anything). Tuck in your shirt and button up except for the neck.

Use your best judgment about a tie. If you're applying for an industry like law enforcement or the financial industry, a tie is highly encouraged. Otherwise, it may not be necessary.

Be well-groomed. Shave your face, cut, wash, and comb or style your hair. Wear deodorant but stay away from cologne because many companies have implemented "no fragrance" policies.

Do not wear jeans or shorts (no matter how nice they look), running shoes or sneakers, V-necks, or casual T-shirts. At a minimum, wear a polo but a button down collar is highly preferable.

If you are having trouble picking out an outfit, type "business casual" for men or women into Google. You'll find tons of examples. Google images will do a way better job of showing you how to dress business casual than I could ever explain to you in a book.

For women, your interview outfit requires clean and wrinkle-free clothes. A simple collared button-down shirt or blouse should be a staple item for an interview, often with dress pants. Conservative colors work well in interviews. Wear a neutral shade of dress pants or a knee-length skirt with a blazer.

A shoe with a modest heel (kitten heels or Mary Janes) is acceptable but avoid open-toed shoes. Keep embellishments, such as bling, buckles, or studs, to a minimum. Wait until after the interview to add more personality into your dress.

Do not wear low-cut shirts, spaghetti straps (or strapless, for that matter), denim, yoga pants, flip flops, or sandals.

In this chapter, I've shown you how to Look good, Feel good, and Play good. You will break necks and cash checks with your business casual style.

In the next chapter, I'll talk about what you should bring to your interview. You'll be prepared for anything that comes your way.

CHAPTER 18

What to Bring to Your Job Interview

Every day without a hire is like a bike without a tire. As long as the tire is missing, the bike isn't going to work as well as it's supposed to. The same theory applies when a company needs to hire.

The company wants to hire fast and will do everything it can to streamline the hiring process. This means that inside the interview invitation, the employer will tell you exactly what documents to bring. If the company does not ask you to bring anything, you are not expected to bring anything.

Bring What's Requested

One thing is for sure: If the hiring manager asks you to bring something, you better bring it.

You may be asked to bring formal identification like your drivers' license and a copy of your cover letter and résumé.

If you're applying for a job in the arts industry, you may be asked to bring a portfolio of artwork or writing samples.

You may also be asked to prepare some kind of presentation on a topic such as solving a challenge the company may be facing. If this is the case, keep your presentation simple and to the point. Focus your entire answer on solving the specific problem the company has asked you to solve.

You may also be asked to perform a skills test during the hiring process. A skills test is a way for the employer to measure your knowledge, skills, aptitudes, or even physical fitness level and can be administered on paper, verbally, or in a designated area for such a test.

What Else to Bring

You generally should bring a pen, a small notebook, and your list of references into the interview.

I highly recommend that you also bring two or three questions to ask the interviewer. Asking questions during the interview will allow you to assess whether this job is right for you. It will show your interest in the position. And it will give you the opportunity to express what you already know about the company. In other words, you're showing you've done your research.

Here is a short list of questions you may consider asking during your next interview:

- What are the day-to-day responsibilities in the first 6 months of the job?
- What is the most important task I should complete in the first 90 days?
- What are some traits of the most successful people already working for your company?

Imagine there are two candidates: One has the questions listed here prepared, and the second has no questions at all. I'd be more willing to engage and follow up with the individual who did have questions over the one who didn't.

Write down your questions on a sheet of paper and bring it to the interview. You can take notes on the answers if you feel it's necessary.

Bring these documents in a professional backpack, briefcase, or laptop bag to ensure there are no creases in any of the papers.

Do Some Research

To create strong questions for your interview, I suggest you research the company to learn more about its customers, products, services, and culture. Research as much information about the employer as possible.

- Where is the company located?
- How many people work there?
- What is the company's mission statement?
- What challenge is this company trying to solve?
- Are there opportunities for advancement at this company?
- Do you know anyone at the company who would refer you for the job?
- Who does this company serve, and how does the company serve that customer?

A few minutes of research will provide you with invaluable information about the company. Use what you learn in your cover letter, résumé, and interview questions.

Now it's time to talk about what's going to happen during your interview!

CHAPTER 19

Your Job Interview: What to Expect

Congratulations. You have received an invitation to interview!

Your cover letter and résumé were strong enough to merit a face-to-face meeting with the company. You have taken great steps to master the art of selling yourself and communicating the value you're going to bring to the company. These are HUGE wins!

Now it's time to dive into what's actually going to happen during your interview. Yes, interviews can be tough, and they can be uncomfortable. But they are necessary.

Objectives

The **company's** objective is to identify a candidate who has **valuable experience** to turn into an employee.

Your objective is to discover **what the company considers valuable** and to **market those specific skills** during the interview.

When these stars align, the interview process is straightforward for all parties involved.

Mindset

I have sat at both sides of the interview table more times than I can count. I have been interviewed for well over 20 jobs and have interviewed hundreds of candidates. Rarely (if ever) has a candidate's education or work experience been the deciding factor in a hire. More often, the candidate's character, honesty, integrity, and willingness to learn and grow are far more important factors than the candidate's degree and experience.

When hiring, I need to know that the candidate will focus on personal and professional growth even when times get tough. I look for candidates who acknowledge that there is always room for improvement, even if they have more than the requested experience for the job.

Bring this mentality to your job interview.

Bring What You Know

No one else can speak to your experience with as much authority as you can.

And remember: The company *wants* to hire you. The company is tired of waiting to hire a worthy candidate. The company wants you to be the solution to its problem.

Relish and enjoy the opportunity to bring what you know to the table. You may be exactly what the company is looking for!

Make Your Best Impression

Please know that the interviewers understand you may be nervous. No one truly enjoys sitting in front of a panel of interviewers and being questioned about employment history. Take a big breath, exhale nice and slow, and enjoy the process.

Following are three traits you should focus on to make the best first impression possible:

1. Friendly personality
2. Professional attitude
3. Organizational and cultural fit

First and foremost, present a friendly personality during the interview. No company desires unfriendly employees, regardless of how talented they are.

Next, be professional. You can be friendly and have great talent, but if you do not manage yourself professionally, the company will not take the risk on you.

Third, you must fit the company culture. It's likely you will not be an organizational fit if you don't meet criteria one and two. But it's possible you're friendly and professional, but don't fit the unique culture of the company. Don't take it the wrong way if you're not a good fit for the culture. It just means the position is not the best for you, and you'll find more opportunities elsewhere.

To determine whether you meet these three traits, the interviewers will be watching for the following:

- How did you demonstrate a friendly personality?
- Were you punctual and honest?
- Did you prepare more than other candidates?
- Did you ask good questions at the end of the interview?
- Do your personal values align with the company's values?
- Do you align with the organization's objectives and purpose?

So, how else can you prepare and show your professionalism?

Be Punctual

Arrive at least 15 minutes early to your interview! Regardless if your interview is in-person or online on Zoom, arrive early. No one wants to hire a NASA scientist who can't make the shuttle launch on time.

Punctuality is just as important as your degree, if not more. If you start off this employment relationship by being late, you can say goodbye to a job offer.

I encourage you to drive (or take the bus) to the interview location before your interview. That way, you'll know how long the drive will take and where you will park once you get there.

Is there a designated parking spot? Do you need to pay for parking? What door will you go in?

Avoid additional stress on interview day by knowing these details before the day of your interview arrives.

Body Language

When the interview starts, greet each interviewer with a firm handshake and a friendly smile. Introduce yourself and then relax.

Remember, you're simply reiterating information you know and have prepared to communicate.

When answering questions, make eye contact with the interviewer. Use the STAR method (see Chapter 16) when responding, and make sure you're answering the question that's been asked. If you need to, ask the interviewer to please repeat the question. It's perfectly acceptable to do that.

Don't read too much into the interviewers' body language or mistake silence for disappointment. During the meeting with you, the interviewers will be "down to business" and will likely be taking notes on your responses. Their focus is hiring, not conversing.

Stay Positive

At the end of the interview, shake hands with the interviewers once again and thank them for their time. Even if you think you bombed the interview, end the interaction on a happy note. Don't leave the interviewers with any kind of negative impression. Leave them with good thoughts about you and your ability to bring results to their company.

Once the interview is over, I suggest following up via email to thank the interviewers for the opportunity. Use this opportunity to explain again how you'll contribute to the company and why you'll be a great fit for the position.

For context, I'd like to share a follow-up email I sent to Omer Redden, Product Manager at Self-Publishing School, after our first 30-minute interview.

I was incredibly excited about this position and really identified with the goals of the company. Hindsight is 20/20, and even now I see ways I could have improved this email.

But I'm so happy I made an effort to communicate my excitement. I wrote:

Good morning, Omer, and happy Thursday!

I want to briefly follow up on yesterday's interview. I was VERY glad to have the opportunity to speak with you.

I can't express enough how much I believe and identify with the goals of SPS, and that is why the opportunity to work for SPS is SO exciting to me. I truly believe we can empower so many people by showing them how to write and publish books. Reading and writing are in the fabric of my character. If you bring me on board, I promise I won't only meet expectations, but I will exceed them with flying colors. I feel like this position was made for me.

The idea of working remotely with an online team is both exciting and inspiring. In my application, I mentioned that I had a 90 WPM typing score, and this fast speed shows just how much the digital world is a part of my life. Communicating remotely with my team in Quebec and with customers around North America has only strengthened my skills in this area. I have the structure, drive, experience, and passion that I know will benefit you and your team.

I have been called an "alpha male without the ego" by a previous employer. This is the kind of "A" player you are looking for—firm but fair, thick skin with a soft heart. I have more than 10 years of customer service experience, have travelled North America visiting customers, and am quite cultured having backpacked Europe and travelled across the United States. I really am a perfect fit.

Again, it was great to meet you. Regardless of the outcome, I wish nothing but the best for you and your team. Thanks!

I focused on over-communicating the skills I have that were listed in the job scorecard, showed lots of excitement, and ended by saying regardless of the outcome of the hiring decision, I was happy for the opportunity. Overall, I ensured there was a positive closure to the entire experience. If I wasn't hired for this position, I'd be in the company's good graces and would likely be considered for another opportunity in the future.

In the next chapter, I'll discuss what to avoid during the interview that could end up costing you the job. Let's take a look.

Chapter 20

Don't Do These Things in Your Interview

Now that you know how to make your interview a success, let's talk about a few things to avoid doing. You've put forth so much effort to build trust with the company, but one misstep can cost you the job.

Stay With Relevant Topics

Chapter 6 covered how important it is not to bring up certain topics in your cover letter, such as political affiliations, religious beliefs, or marital status. Leave these things out of the interview, too.

I am not suggesting you dismiss your character or beliefs. Nor am I intending to persuade you to leave who you are as a person out of the discussion. The reason I make this suggestion is twofold.

First, your number one aim during an interview is to land the job. Discuss only the most relevant topics related to employment history and value to the company. This is not the time or place for anything else.

Second, we all know these topics can ignite passionate responses from people. It's best to focus on what value you'll bring to the company as a qualified professional. Once you've landed the job, you'll have all the time in the world to discuss what makes you *you*.

Maintain a professional demeanor throughout the entire hiring process, but especially during the interview. Be friendly, but don't mistake the interviewers for your dear old friends. You may get along well with the interviewers, but always maintain professionalism.

Absolute No-No's

Swearing is a major red flag for the interviewers. Have fun and enjoy the experience, but don't swear.

Integrity is a significant factor in the hiring process. So, never lie about your work experience or the qualifications you hold. It's hard to build back trust, and you may never have another opportunity to do so. Lying about your qualifications or experience also can blacklist you from future employment opportunities.

Do not bring your cell phone to the interview. Leave it in the car, or at home, or with your significant other. It is extremely unprofessional for your phone to go off in the middle of your interview. **Do not** be that person who says, "Oh shoot, I forgot to turn it off!"

Do not, under any circumstance, speak badly about or blame others when relating past work experiences. You'll likely be asked about a time you had a difficult situation with a coworker. When you do, take extreme ownership over your professional career. Hiring managers do not have respect for candidates who do not take accountability for their actions.

The Right Salary

If you're asked to bring a salary requirement to your interview, do not provide a single number. Instead, provide a researched wage range.

Go to a site called Glassdoor* to research the average industry wage for the job you're applying for. Review a minimum of three different companies with the position you're applying for to find an average wage in the industry. Be sure to account for job location when researching average salaries because wages can vary significantly from city to city.

Providing a salary range allows the employer some room to negotiate, and you avoid selling yourself short. After doing your research, you'll also feel confident knowing *real* wage expectations for the position.

Be Yourself

Be genuine and honest throughout your job-search process. Your unique perspective and character can be exactly what the company is looking for. Being anyone other than yourself will flat-out set you up for failure.

There you have it. Now you know exactly what not to do in your interview. You can avoid problematic conversations that may prevent you from landing your dream job.

BONUS CONTENT

The 1-Hour Job Application Challenge

1-Hour Job Application Challenge
CHECKLIST

Read Job Description ☑
Write Cover Letter ☑
Write Résumé ☑
Prep for Interview ☑

Step 1: Read and understand the job description or job scorecard.

Understanding the job description or job scorecard will help you focus your application on the skills that provide the most value for the company. If a company is looking for skills X, Y, and Z, a strong job application will show your work experience (and the results you've produced) using skills X, Y, and Z. This way, you align the experience you have with what the hiring manager needs to make a hiring decision.

Most candidates fail to make this connection for the employer.

Job Description / Job Scorecard Action Plan:

1. Print out the job description or job scorecard for the job you are applying for. Yes, actually print it.

2. Underline any "required" certifications or experience. These are must-haves for the employer and **need** to be referenced in your cover letter and résumé.

3. Out of the remaining "preferred" skills and experience listed in the job description, ask yourself:

    o   What items provide the most value to the employer?

    o   What items have the most impact toward the success of the role?

    o   What items do I have the most experience doing?

    Underline three to five items. These are the certifications, skills, and experience you will target in your cover letter and résumé.

    Skills beyond your top five do not deserve to take up real estate in your cover letter.

4. Take note of any special instructions that need to be included in your application.

Step 2: Write your cover letter.

A cover letter is a one-page document used to entice an employer to hire you. Illuminate your passion and desire for the position while highlighting your most relevant qualifications for the job by using information from the job description or job scorecard.

It's critical to make every sentence in your cover letter count toward marketing yourself and your skills. Hook your future boss's attention by showing how your experience will bring value to the company.

A cover letter consists of four main sections:

1. The company's contact information
2. The introductory paragraph
3. The main body where you'll communicate your skills
4. The closing paragraph

Do not include pictures, information regarding marital status, sexual preference, religious affiliations, or political leanings in your cover letter or résumé.

And remember . . .

Explain what you can do for the employer, NOT what the employer can do for you.

Cover Letter Action Step:

The Company's Contact Information

1. At the top of a blank Google or Word doc, type the contact information of the company you are applying to. This includes the name of the company, street address, city, and state or province, each on its own line.

2. Leave two lines blank below the company's contact info. Then direct your cover letter to the hiring manager. For example, "Attn: Michael Lachance."

The Introductory Paragraph

1. Leave a single line blank.

2. Your introduction will be three sentences long:

   a. In the first sentence, state what job you are applying for. If there is a job number on the job description or job scorecard, include it here. If you were referred to this job by someone who works for the company, include that person's name and job title here.

   b. In the second sentence, include one or two skills, certifications, or educational experiences you have that will stand out to the employer. Capture the employer's attention and give the company a reason to continue learning more about you.

    c.   In the third sentence, state that you have the experience and skills needed to excel in this position. Make it obvious. Explain how you will benefit the company and bring value to its team.

The Main Body

1. In section three of your cover letter, write a paragraph targeting the three to five skills you identified in the job description or job scorecard. The employer needs to understand how you've used these skills to bring value in your employment history. Explain how you will apply your experience toward the skills the company needs.

The Closing Paragraph

1. Your closing paragraph should be three sentences long:

    a.   Thank the employer for considering your application.

    b.   List your phone number and email, and encourage the employer to contact you.

    c.   Invite the employer to learn more about you by reading your résumé.

2. Lastly, leave a single blank line space and on the next line type, "Sincerely," followed by your signature and then your typed name.

3. Type "Enclosed: Résumé (2)" at the very bottom of the page. This tells the employer you have two (2) résumé pages that go with your cover letter.

Step 3: Write your résumé.

A résumé is a professional document used to showcase your employability when applying for a job. It includes your contact information, education, employment, and volunteer experience, and any awards or certifications you've received that describe who you are as a professional candidate.

Résumé Action Step:

Your Contact Information

1. Type your **contact information** in the Header of a blank Word doc and center align the text. On the first line, type your first and last name. Bold the text and increase the font size. Your name will be the largest text size on your résumé.

2. On the second line, type your street address, city, state or province, and ZIP or country code.

3. On the third line, type your phone number and email address.

4. On the fourth line, use the underscore key to create a line that will serve as a visual break between your Contact Information and your Education section.

5. Review the example below.

Michael Lachance
Address, City, Province/State, Postal/Zip Code
Cell: (123) 456-7890 Email: michancebooks@gmail.com

Education

1. Bold, underline, and caps lock the word **<u>EDUCATION</u>**. This is your Education section header. Leave a single blank line underneath.

2. Next, type the most recent education degree you've received, and bold the text.

3. On the same line, aligned at the far-right side of the page, type the date range of when you went to school for this degree.

4. On the next line, use the bulleted list format and type the name of the university, college, or high school you graduated from, including the city and state or province.

5. Repeat this process for all the degrees you intend to list on your résumé.

6. Review the example below.

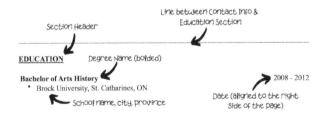

Employment Experience

1. Bold, underline, and caps lock the words **EMPLOYMENT EXPERIENCE.** This is your Employment Experience section header. Leave a single blank line underneath.
2. Next, type your most recent job title and bold it.
3. On the same line, aligned at the far-right side of the page, type the date range of when you began and ended employment for this job. If you are still working for this company, type "Present" instead of an end date.
4. Underneath your job title, in regular font, type the name of the company you work(ed) for, including the company's location (city and state or province).

You will NOT land your dream job listing duties on your résumé.

A common mistake job candidates make is listing only the duties or tasks performed at a job. Listing a duty such as "tracked inventory" or "fulfilled customer orders" does not paint a picture of how you brought value, results, or achievements to the company. The hiring manager will not see any value in you as a candidate and you will not be hired.

Whenever possible, use quantitative measurements to best express your value.

Numbers are objective, measurable, and the best weapon you have when creating your cover letter and résumé.

Achievement Statements allow you to communicate the results you've provided in structured sentences. Each job title you include on your résumé should have three to five Achievement Statements, and ideally, each statement should focus on a result listed in the job description or job scorecard.

Here is the Achievement Statement formula:

Action word (past tense) + **context** (what you did / who you did it for) + **achievement** (results you achieved)

5. On the next line, use the Achievement Statement formula to write Achievement sentences.
   a. Use a new bullet point for every Achievement Statement.
   b. Focus each Achievement Statement on a different skill from the job description or job scorecard.
6. Review the example below.

EMPLOYMENT EXPERIENCE

Student Success Representative   March 2018 – Present
Self-Publishing School, San Francisco, California
- Created a Self-Publishing School Help Center that reduced the number of Support Tickets for the Student Success team by more than 90%
- Refined an Accounts Receivable campaign, resulting in $15,000 in past-due collections every month
- Systematized daily procedures and activities to increase efficiency, which merited the 2018 "Playbook Beast Q4" award in recognition of those efforts

Volunteer Experience

1. Include this section if you have volunteer experience that would be valuable to the employer. Bold, underline, and caps lock the words **VOLUNTEER EXPERIENCE**. This is your Volunteer Experience section header. Leave a single blank line underneath.

2. Type your most recent volunteer position title and bold it.

3. On the same line, aligned at the far-right side of the page, type the date range of when you began and ended volunteering for this organization. If you are still volunteering, type "Present" instead of an end date.

4. Under your volunteer title in regular font, type the name of the organization you volunteer(ed) for, including its location (city, state or province).

5. Each volunteer position you include on your résumé should have two to three Achievement Statements, and ideally, each sentence should focus on a skill or result listed in the job description or job scorecard.

6. Review the example below.

VOLUNTEER EXPERIENCE

Choices Program Volunteer   March 2018 – May 2018
Sarnia-Lambton Rebound, Sarnia, ON
- Dedicated 2 hours weekly to support Sarnia-Lambton Rebound and positively impact local community
- Engaged in positive discussions with youth, focusing on substance abuse, prevention, and intervention techniques to help them make more informed decisions

Professional Development

1. Include this section if you have completed training or have certifications that are required by or would be valuable to the employer. If you don't have any professional development to include in your résumé, you may want to choose to add a Workshops, Awards, or Certifications section instead of Professional Development.

   Bold, underline, and caps lock the words **<u>PROFESSIONAL DEVELOPMENT</u>**. This is your Professional Development section header. Professional certifications, aptitude tests, language tests, publications, job-related training, health and safety training, and advanced qualifications can all go here. Leave a single blank line underneath.

2. Next, type the name of the most recent training you've received or have been certified in.

3. On the same line, aligned at the far-right side of the page, type the date of when you received the training or were certified. Include only the year unless the certification is time-bound.

4. Repeat this process for any other professional development certifications you intend to include on your résumé.

5. Review the example below.

PROFESSIONAL DEVELOPMENT/WORKSHOPS

Michael Hyatt's "The Focused Leader" Training	2019
Copywriting Mastery - Digital Marketer HQ	2018
Student Success TedX Talk - Presentation Training	2018

Step 4: Prepare for your interview.

It's time to prepare for your interview so you can land your dream job!

Let's start off with a philosophy called the Seven Ps. The Seven Ps are: **P**roper **P**rior **P**lanning **P**revents **P**iss **P**oor **P**erformance.

Proper prior planning will prevent you from giving a piss poor performance. The problem is that most candidates do not prepare for their interview nearly as much as they should. When the day comes, Peter Procrastinator ends up feeling stressed and anxious because he has not properly prepared.

In the interview stage, the **company's** objective is to identify a candidate who has **valuable experience** to turn into an employee.

Your objective in the interview stage is to discover **what the company considers valuable** and to **market those specific skills** during the interview.

When these stars align, the interview process is straightforward for all parties involved.

There are two common types of interview questions you can begin preparing for today.

Behavior-Based Questions

The first kind is the **behavioral-based question.** Behavioral-based questions explore your behaviors when dealing with different situations from your past.

Following are 10 common behavioral-based interview questions. Even though you'll tell a story from your past, respond in a way that will provide value to the employer in the future.

1. Give an example of a time you faced conflict while working as part of a team.
2. What do you do if you disagree with someone at work?
3. Have you ever made a mistake at work? How did you handle it?
4. Give an example of a time you had to take on the role of a leader.
5. Tell me about a time you worked effectively under pressure.
6. Describe a time you didn't meet the expectations of your manager.
7. Have you experienced a stressful situation? How did you deal with it?

8. Share an example of how you were able to motivate employees or coworkers.

9. Have you ever gone beyond the call of duty? If so, how?

10. How do you handle a challenge? Give an example.

Competency-Based Questions

The second type of interview question is the **competency-based interview question.** These questions determine whether you have the experience and skill for the job you're applying for.

1. Give an example of a time when you led a team. What did you accomplish?

2. Describe a time you've used effective time management to complete a project.

3. Tell me about a time you failed to complete a project on time.

4. Tell me about a time your communication skills helped improve a situation.

5. Tell me about a time you responded to negative customer feedback.

6. Describe a situation where you had to deal with an angry customer.

7. Describe a time you performed a task you'd never done before.

8. What is your biggest achievement?

9. Tell me about a time you failed to communicate properly. Looking back, what would you have done differently?

10. Give an example of a time you identified a new approach to a workplace problem.

Use the STAR Method

To maximize the value of your responses, use the STAR method. This method can be very effective in helping you structure your responses, and it breaks down as follows:

Star: Describe the Situation.

Task: Describe the Task required of you.

Action: Describe the Actions you took.

Result: Describe the Results of your actions.

First, you describe the problem or situation you were facing. Next, you explain the task, or what you had to do to correct the situation. You then explain the actions you took to make the change happen. Finally, you describe the results of your actions.

A Job Seeker in Your Life
Needs Your Help!

I'm grateful to be in a position where I can share my 10+ years of employment experience with you.

But one major problem remains:

Other job candidates are struggling to land *their* dream job.

That's why I really need your help.

There is someone in your social network who is struggling to secure employment and create a stable financial future for themselves.

Whether it be one of your friends, family members, roommates or classmates, you have the opportunity to change their employment destiny right now.

Ask them to go to the link below to receive free Land Your Dream Job content:

bit.ly/lydjresources

They'll receive the entire 1-Hour Job Application Challenge chapter, the cover letter and résumé samples from this book, along with more job-search strategy tips absolutely free.

Don't wait! You can help change a job seeker's employment status, today!

Urgent Plea :)

Thank You SO Much for Reading My Book!

I really appreciate all your feedback, and I love hearing what you have to say.

Please leave me a helpful review on Amazon, letting me know what you thought of the book.

Simply go to **bit.ly/lydjreview** and click "Write a customer review."

Thanks again!

–Michael Lachance

Ready to Turn Your Passion into Your Dream Job?

Thanks to Self-Publishing School, I've been able to turn my knowledge, my experience, and my passions into a self-published book.

By self-publishing, I've...

Created an additional income stream for myself

Built credibility in the employment industry

Changed lives, one job-seeker at a time

Learned about sales, marketing, and leveraged impact

And equipped myself with invaluable entrepreneurial skills.

Learn how to turn YOUR experience into a book by going to **self-publishingschool.com/friend**

Add my name as the referral, and I'll make sure a copy of Chandler Bolt's book

Published: The Proven Path from Blank Page to Published Author

is sent to you, absolutely free.

Made in the USA
Coppell, TX
25 March 2021

52251965R10085